The Most Exciting Breakthrough to Date in Mastering One of the Most Vital Skills in Today's World

Here is the first program based on the actual functioning of the human brain and eyes as established by modern research. Building upon this foundation, it allows you to dramatically increase your reading speed and comprehension with an ease and efficiency never before deemed possible. This updated Third Edition of SPEED READING is the perfect handbook—a classic work on the subject that is ideal for students, teachers, executives, and anyone eager to improve the speed, comprehension, and quality of their reading. The results are guaranteed.

TONY BUZAN is one of the world's leading authorities on the brain and learning techniques. His training companies advise top- and middle-management executives of such corporations as IBM and Mobil. In addition, a number of widely hailed television programs have been created around his learning techniques, among them the famed ten-part BBC series "Use Your Head," which served as the basis for his global bestseller, *Use Both Sides of Your Brain*.

BOOKS, VIDEOS AND AUDIO TAPES BY TONY BUZAN

Books
Master Your Memory
Memory Vision (workbook for Master Your Memory)
Use Both Sides of Your Brain
Use Your Perfect Memory
The Brain User's Guide
Make the Most of Your Mind
Harnessing the ParaBrain
(Business version of Make the Most of Your Mind)
Spore One (poetry – Limited Edition)

Video Tapes
Use Your Head
The Enchanted Loom
Buzan Business Brain Training
Developing Family Genius

Audio Tapes
Learning and Memory
The Intelligence Revolution
Make the Most of Your Mind
Supercreativity and Mind Mapping

Other Works
The Universal Personal Organiser
'Body and Soul' (Master Mind Map Poster)
The Mind Map Kit
Master Your Memory Matrix (SEM^3) 0-10,000

See Appendix for more information
including how to order these items

THIRD EDITION

SPEED READING

State-of-the-art techniques to improve your reading speed and comprehension—based on the latest discoveries about the human brain

TONY BUZAN

COMPLETELY REVISED AND UPDATED

A PLUME BOOK

DEDICATION

To my dear, dear Mum, who so lovingly and so caringly introduced me to the beauty and power of the word; the beauty and the power of the mind.

External editor-in-chief, Vanda North

PLUME
Published by the Penguin Group
Penguin Books USA Inc., 375 Hudson Street, New York, New York 10014, U.S.A.
Penguin Books Ltd, 27 Wrights Lane, London W8 5TZ, England
Penguin Books Australia Ltd, Ringwood, Victoria, Australia
Penguin Books Canada Ltd, 10 Alcorn Avenue, Toronto, Ontario, Canada M4V 3B2
Penguin Books (N.Z.) Ltd, 182-190 Wairau Road, Auckland 10, New Zealand

Penguin Books Ltd, Registered Offices: Harmondsworth, Middlesex, England

Published by Plume, an imprint of New American Library, a division of Penguin Books USA Inc. Simultaneously published in a Dutton hardcover edition.

First Plume Printing, January, 1991
10

 REGISTERED TRADEMARK—MARCA REGISTRADA

Mind Mapping is a registered trademark of the Buzan Organization, 1990.

LIBRARY OF CONGRESS CATALOGING-IN-PUBLICATION DATA

Buzan, Tony.
    Speed reading/Tony Buzan.—3rd ed.
        p.   cm.

    ISBN 0-452-26604-1
    1. Rapid reading.   I. Title.
LB1050.54.B89   1991
428.4'3—dc20   90-19572
                                                                              CIP

BOOKS ARE AVAILABLE AT QUANTITY DISCOUNTS WHEN USED TO PROMOTE PRODUCTS OR SERVICES. FOR INFORMATION PLEASE WRITE TO PREMIUM MARKETING DIVISION, PENGUIN BOOKS USA INC., 375 HUDSON STREET, NEW YORK, NEW YORK 10014.

CONTENTS

EDITOR'S FOREWORD

It is a privilege to commend this book to the great army of people, young and old, who are eager to master more knowledge of our exasperating and endearing world – the heritage of the past, scientific and political developments of the day, current and classical literature. It marks the emergence of a brilliant young man, Tony Buzan, whose career I have, in a modest way, been trying to foster for several years and who has rapidly made a name for himself.

Tony Buzan here reduces to a simple and easily followed learning system what I and my contemporaries had to acquire painfully and empirically – if we acquired it at all. Let me assure you that using this system you will swiftly equal if not exceed what I have had to do for many years: read at least three newspapers a day; some 25 scientific journals, half a dozen general weeklies and two or three books each week; and about a dozen general magazines each month – as well as many letters, reports, clippings, references, handbooks, catalogues, etc.

I could wish that I had years ago enjoyed the benefit of the system Tony Buzan here sets forth so lucidly. It would have saved me much lost effort, many wasted moves; and I am not a bit ashamed to admit that even today I continue to learn from him how to do still better. You are likely to have the advantage of starting out on the right foot at a much earlier stage. I plead with you to seize the opportunity! It will require effort, even with Tony Buzan's clearly explained step-by-step system; but if you persevere, you will find that this book is like the opening of a door into a world thick with the golden sunshine of knowledge.

HEINZ NORDEN
Erstwhile Information Editor, The Book of Knowledge
Fellow of the Institute of Linguistics
1974

PART ONE

ABOUT READING

Learning to speed read effortlessly and fluently has been claimed by millions of people around the world to be one of the most rewarding and significant events of their lives.

As most readers will be aware the field of speed reading itself has contributed to the recent print explosion. Almost as soon as we were swamped with books to read, we were swamped with books on how to read them. Unfortunately many of these books were written by people with no real qualification in the fields of Education, Psychology, and Reading in particular. This book will therefore take issue with much of what has been published up to the present time, and will present new theories and explanations on such major areas as vocalising while reading, study methods, back-skipping and regression, finger-pointing, skimming and scanning, and comprehension. A number of other out-of-date concepts will be explained in the light of the most recent research on the brain, and the new concept of Speed and Range Reading.

Whereas traditional speed reading encourages you simply to go faster and faster, Speed and Range Reading shows you how to *read at any speed you wish to from 1–20,000 words per minute, dependent entirely upon your own reading goals.* The Speed and Range reader is not forced to dash over every word of print, in the same way that the finely-trained athlete is not obliged to sprint everywhere he goes.

As with the athlete, the Speed and Range readers *can* sprint and *can* stroll, and because they are finely-trained/tuned will be able to do everything more efficiently, easily and skilfully.

Modern research has shown that your eye-brain system is thousands of times more complex and powerful than had previously been estimated, and that with proper training you can quickly reap the benefits of this enormous potential.

The essay in Self Test 1 – *The Intelligence War – at the Front with Brain Training*, will give you a comprehensive guide and overview to this latest research, and you are advised to note the main elements of this essay, bearing them in mind as you read through *Speed Reading*. By so doing you will be able to put everything into context, and thus increase the speed with which your speed and comprehension increase!

In Speed and Range Reading you will thus be learning to use the entire range of your cortical skills. (See *Use Both Sides of Your Brain,* by the author.)

Thus when you read in the comprehensive way outlined in *Speed Reading*, you will be using not only your words, sequential abilities and logic, but also, as you read, your imagination, rhythm, and even, where appropriate, your daydreaming capacity.

Speed Reading will guarantee that you develop a 'whole brain' approach to reading, while at the same time increasing your overall general knowledge in the Self-Test sections, which deal with:

1. The Intelligence War
2. Psychology
3. The Methods of Science
4. The Major Musical Instruments
5. History – The Prehistoric Period
6. Art – Primitive to Christian
7. Art – Gothic to National Schools
8. Astronomy
9. The History of Communications
10. The Enchanted Loom – Your Brain

Reading – A Necessity
In recent years the volume of magazines and books pouring off the international presses has reached almost unmanageable proportions, and a number of steps must be taken to meet this rising flood.

The History of Speed Reading

The early development of speed reading can be traced to the beginning of this century, when the publication explosion swamped readers with more than they could possibly handle at normal reading rates. Most early courses, however, were based on information provided from a rather unexpected source – the Air Force.

Air Force tacticians had noticed that a number of pilots were, when flying, unable to distinguish planes seen at a distance. In the life-and-death situation of combat, this inability was obviously an enormous disadvantage, and the Air Force psychologists and educationalists set about finding a remedy for the situation. They developed a machine called a tachistoscope, which is simply a device for flashing images for varying instants of time on a large screen. They started by flashing fairly large pictures of friendly and enemy aircraft at very slow exposures and then gradually shortened the exposure while decreasing the size of the image seen. They found to their surprise that with training, the average person was able to distinguish almost specklike representations of different planes when the images had been flashed on the screen for only one five-hundredth of a second.

Reasoning that the perceptual ability of the eyes had been vastly underrated, they decided to transfer this information to reading. Using exactly the same device and process, they first flashed one large word for as long as five seconds on a screen, gradually reducing the size of the word and shortening the length of the flash. This they were able to do until they were flashing four words simultaneously on a screen for one five-hundredth of a second, and were still able to obtain recognition.

As a consequence of this approach, most speed-reading courses and kits were based on tachistoscopic training.

This approach usually provided the student with a graph graded in units of ten from one hundred to four hundred words per minute (see figure opposite above). Most people, with regular training, were able to climb from an average of two hundred per minute to an average of four hundred per minute. Unfortunately, the graduates of such training

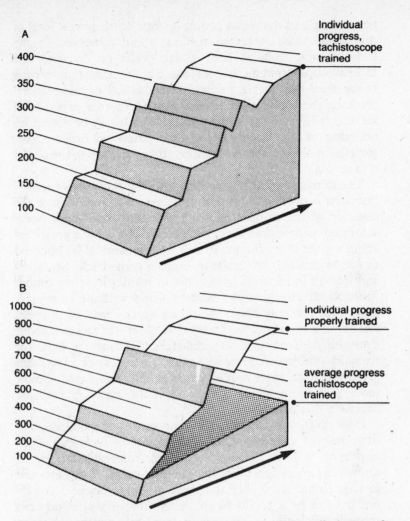

Fig. 1 A. Tachistoscopic graph. B. Measuring the relative effectiveness of tachistoscopic training

schemes reported a general dissatisfaction after a few weeks of 'postgraduate reading'. An enormous number of them noticed that shortly after the course had finished, their reading speed once again sank to its previous level.

Only recently was it realized that the *normal range* of reading ability is from roughly two hundred to four hundred words per minute and that most people operate at the lowest level of this range. The increased reading ability observed in the tachistoscopic courses had in fact little to do with the tachistoscopic training, but was more a function of motivation being eked out over a period of weeks and of the readers' reaching the top of their normal range. Another explanation for the failure of the still-screen approach can be found by referring to the basic rule of observation: in order to see something clearly, the eye must be still in relation to the object it is seeing.

The fantastic growth of reading material is obvious enough, but what is overlooked is that there are *no known limits* to the capacity of the human mind. There are today more 'well-informed' people than ever, i.e. people who know a great deal about a great many things. In fact, the 'generalist' (as opposed to the 'specialist') has made a startling come-back. Scientists and leaders in all fields have come to realise that they cannot function effectively in the modern world without knowing a great deal not only about their own special field of interest, but about a broad range of related subjects – in fact just about everything. Yesterday's specialist, defined as 'a man (or woman) who knows more and more about less and less,' has given way to an eager host of young people who want to 'know more and more about more and more' and are realising precisely this ambition.

How do they do it? It is not just a matter of mobilising the huge reserve capacity of the human mind. *Technique* is all-important – how to absorb, master, integrate and retain knowledge most expeditiously and efficiently. A key element in acquiring these skills it to *increase reading efficiency*. You do not have to be a genius to appreciate that if you could read twice as efficiently as you now do, you could go through twice as much reading material in the same time.

It goes without saying that 'speed'-reading is utterly pointless if you *do not understand or cannot remember what you read*. All speed-reading methods recognise that and use so-called 'Comprehension tests' to check that you actually have understood and retained what you have read, to make certain that your comprehension keeps pace with your growing speed. Quite apart from important improvements in the technique of learning how to read fast which are set forth in this book, what I wish to emphasise in my system is that *understanding and remembering factual material* is not nearly as important as knowing how to *relate new material to what you already know*. This is the all-important 'integrative factor', or if you will, *learning how to learn*. You cannot 'look up' *perspective, interrelation, or how to make a consistent, coherent meaningful pattern of everything you know and learn*. It is how you put them together, how you use them, that counts in getting ahead in the modern science-oriented world.

This book will teach you how to read faster and with a greater range of speeds, and also how to make something of everything you have ever read or will ever read.

Self Tests and Exercises
The special exercises in certain chapters are designed to increase your facility in visual perception, mental awareness and critical ability. There is also a programmed series of articles and selected readings designed to give you a continuing indication of your progress through the book.

These readings are a series dealing with the theories and history of the major areas of human knowledge. By the time you have finished the book you will therefore not only have increased your reading speed, maintained your comprehension, and improved your critical and appreciative abilities, but also will have been given a very good general education.

How to Read
Having mentioned the print explosion and the similar explosion in better reading books, I have now added to that total myself. To atone for this sin I offer an approach to Speed and Range Reading which will aid you to complete it as efficiently as possible.

Having read the preface, go through the table of contents thoroughly, mapping out the territory you wish to cover. Then roughly plan the time period you will devote to each section of the book, finishing with a general outline in your mind's eye of both the content and the programme of study for that content.

After this, browse quickly through the book, familiarising

SPEED READING GRAPH

	1	2	3	4	5	6	7	8	9	10
100% / 2400										
95% / 2200										
90% / 2000										
85% / 1800										
80% / 1600										
75% / 1400										
70% / 1200										
65% / 1000										
60% / 800										
55% / 600										
50% / 400										
45% / 200										
40% / 0										
35%										
30%										
25%										
20%										
15%										
10%										

Comprehension Speed

Test Number

yourself with the different sections, and adding to the mental picture already developed by the table of contents. Before each chapter-reading a quick refresher-browse will help to re-familiarise you with the material that is about to be covered, and will make the whole reading task far easier and more enjoyable.

Try to complete one chapter every 3 days, practising your newly acquired techniques in the intervening time periods between chapters. To give you some basic signposts to reading performance, the following table is provided:

	Reader	Speed	Comprehension
1	Poor	10–100 wpm	30–50%
2	Average	200–240 wpm	50–70%
3	Functionally literate	400 wpm	70–80%
4	Top 1%	800–1000 wpm	80+%
5	Top .01%	1000+ wpm	80+%

To aid you in reaching your own goals within these para-meters, a special graph for your speed and comprehension has been included on page 14. To help you calculate your speed more rapidly, the number of words in each of the self tests has been noted at the beginning of the test. In order to calculate your words per minute, simply divide the number of words by the number of minutes you took to read the passage.

To calculate your percentage comprehension, divide the number of correct answers by 15. To give you a rough guide, 15 correct gives you 100% comprehension; 10 correct gives you 66%. Then, record your speed score in one colour (or with an 'X') and your comprehension score in another colour (or with a different symbol) in the test number column.

And don't worry about how 'bad' a reader you may be at the beginning – a recent survey showed that, after leaving formal education, the average person read one new book per year, of which they had forgotten 80% within two weeks, increased their vocabulary by an average of only three words per year, learnt one new subject per life, and on average no new languages. By the time you have finished Speed and Range Reading you will be 'world class' in each of these categories!

CHAPTER ONE

THE STARTING POINT – CHECK YOUR NORMAL READING SPEED AND COMPREHENSION

In any learning or self-improvement situation, it is essential to find the true base from which you start. There is no right or wrong, good or bad in this, only an accurate assessment of where you are positioned in the present. Whatever that position is, it will form a solid foundation from which you will be able to springboard successfully to your ultimate goal.

In this chapter I ask you to do exactly the opposite of what I shall be asking you to do in every other chapter. I ask you *not* to speed, because this reading is to give an indication of what your normal reading speed is. If you go faster than you are accustomed to you will not be able to judge accurately the progress you make throughout the book, and will not really know your present reading level. Comprehension will also be tested. It should be the kind of comprehension you get when normally reading this type of material.

Don't worry about getting low scores in either speed *or* comprehension. Remember that this book has been written for people who want to improve their reading skills and that low initial scores are not only common, they're expected.

So no dashing along for higher than usual speeds, no plodding for super comprehension scores, and no worrying about your result. Have your watch by your side, do your reading privately (someone timing you or watching you inevitably disturbs comprehension and tends to make some people read more hurriedly than usual, others more slowly) and start a *normal* reading on the following passage *now*.

SELF TEST 1
THE INTELLIGENCE WAR –
AT THE FRONT WITH BRAIN TRAINING

New World Trends

Stock Market analysts watch, like hawks, ten individuals in Silicon Valley. When there is even a hint that one might move from Company A to Company B, the world's stock markets shift.

The English Manpower Services Commission recently published a survey in which it was noted that of the top 10% of British companies, 80% invested considerable money and time in training; and of the bottom 10% of companies no money or time was invested.

In Minnesota, the Plato computer education project has already raised the thinking and academic performance levels of 200,000 pupils.

In the armed forces of an increasing number of countries, Mental Martial Arts are becoming as important as physical combat skills.

National Olympic squads are devoting as much as 30% of their training time to the development of mental set, stamina, and visualisation.

In the Fortune 500, the top five computer companies alone have spent over a billion dollars on educating their employees.

In Caracas, Dr. Luis Alberto Machado became the first human being to be given a Government portfolio as Minister of Intelligence, with a political mandate to raise the level of the mental power of a nation.

We are witnessing the explosive embryonic growth of a new Quantum Leap in evolution – the awareness by intelligence of itself, and the concomitant awareness that that intelligence can be nurtured to astounding advantage.

This encouraging news must be considered in the context of the problem areas defined by the business community as most significant.

The information from the Brain Front must then be applied to these main areas.

Over the last twenty years over 100,000 people were polled, and on each of the five continents. Among the more than 100 mental skill areas commonly mentioned as requiring improvement, the top 20 are:

Memory
Concentration
Communication – presentation skills/public speaking
Communication – presentation skills/written
Creative thinking
Planning
Thought organisation
Problem analysis
Problem solving
Motivation
Analytical thinking
Prioritising
Reading speed (volume of material to be read)
Reading comprehension
Time management
Stress
Fatigue
Assimilation of information
Getting started (procrastination)
Declining mental ability with age

Each of these areas can be, with the aid of modern research on the functioning of the brain, tackled with relative ease. This modern research includes:

1. Left and right cortex research;
2. Mind Mapping;
3. Super-speed and Range reading/Intellectual Commando Units;
4. Mnemonic techniques;
5. Memory loss after learning;
6. Your brain cell;
7. Mental abilities and age.

Left and Right Cortical Research
It has now become common knowledge that the left and right cortical structures of the brain dominantly deal with different

intellectual functions. The left cortex primarily handles logic, words, number, sequence, analysis, linearity and listing, while the right cortex processes rhythm, colour, imagination, day dreaming and spatial relationships, dimension and Gestalt.

What has recently been realised is that the left cortex is not the 'academic' side, nor is the right cortex the 'creative, intuitive, emotional' side. We now know from volumes of research that both sides need to be used in conjunction with each other for there to be both academic and creative success.

The Einsteins, Newtons, Cezannes, and Mozarts of this world, like the great business geniuses, combined their linguistic, numerical and analytical skills with imagination and visualising in order to produce their creative masterpieces.

Mind Mapping

Using this basic knowledge of our functioning, it is possible to train personnel in skills relating to each of the problem areas, often producing incremental improvements of 500%.

One of the modern methods for achieving such improvement is Mind Mapping.

In traditional note taking, whether it be for memory, for the preparation of communication, for the organisation of thought, for problem analysis, for planning or for creative thinking, the standard mode is linear: either sentences, short phrase lists, or numerically and alphabetically ordered lists. These methods, because of their lack of colour, visual rhythm, image and spatial relationships, cauterise the brain's thinking capacities, and are literally counter-productive to each of the aforementioned processes.

Mind Mapping uses the full range of the brain's abilities, placing an image in the centre of the page in order to facilitate memorisation and the creative generation of ideas, and subsequently branching out in associative networks that mirror externally the brain's internal structures. By using this approach, the preparation of speeches can be reduced in time terms from days to minutes; problems can be solved both more comprehensively and more rapidly; memory can be improved from absent to perfect; and creative thinkers can generate a limitless number of ideas rather than a truncated list.

Super-Speed and Range Reading/Intellectual Commando units

Combining Mind Mapping with new super-speed and range reading techniques that allow speeds of well over 1,000 words per minute in conjunction with excellent comprehension, and eventual *effective* reading speeds of about 10,000 words per minute, one can form Intellectual Commando Units.

Reading at these advanced speeds, Mind Mapping in detail the outline of the book and its chapters, and exchanging the information gathered by using advanced Mind Mapping and presentation skills, it is possible for four or more individuals to acquire, integrate, memorise and begin to apply in their professional situation four complete books' worth of new information in one day.

These techniques have recently been applied in the multi-national organisations, Nabisco and Digital Computers. In these instances, 40 and 120 senior executives divided their groups into four. Each individual in each of the four sub-groups spent two hours applying Speed and Range Reading techniques to one of the four selected books.

When the two hours were completed, the members of each sub-group discussed among themselves their understandings, interpretations and reactions to the book. Each sub-group then chose one 'representative' who gave a comprehensive lecture to all the members of the three other sub-groups. This process was repeated four times, and at the end of each respective day, 40 and 120 senior executives walked out of their seminar room with four complete new books-worth of information in their heads, and not only *in* their heads, but integrated, analysed and memorised.

This approach can be similarly used in the family situation, and is already being so used in families around the world.

In one recent instance, a Mexican family applied it to their three children, ranging in age from 6 to 15. Within a year, each child was the top student in its year, having been able to complete in two days with the help of the other family members, what the average child/student completes in a year.

The implications are obvious.

For more detailed information of this approach and the Mind Map Organic Study Technique see *Harnessing the*

Parabrain for business application, and *Make the Most of Your Mind* for family application (by the author).

Mnemonic Techniques

Mnemonic techniques were originally invented by the Greeks, and were thought to be 'tricks'. We now realise that these devices are soundly based on the brain's functioning, and that when applied appropriately they can dramatically improve any memory performance.

In the mnemonic techniques one uses the principles of association and imagination, making dramatic, colourful, sensual and consequently unforgettable images in one's mind.

The Mind Map is in fact a multi-dimensional mnemonic, using the brain's innate functional areas to more effectively imprint required data/information upon itself.

Using mnemonics businessmen have been trained to remember perfectly 40 newly introduced people, and to similarly memorise lists of over 100 products, facts and data. These techniques are now being applied at the IBM Training Centre in Stockholm, and have majorly impacted the success of their 17-week introductory training programme.

This awareness that learning how to learn *before* any other training has been given makes particularly good business sense, which is why a number of the more progressive international organisations are now making it the obligatory 'front end' to all their training courses. Simple calculation shows that if £1,000,000 is spent on training, and 80% of that training is forgotten within two weeks, £800,000 has been lost during that same period!

Memory Loss After Learning

Memory loss after learning is dramatic.

After a one hour learning period, there is a short rise in the recall of information as the brain integrates the new data, which is followed by a dramatic decline in which, by the end of 24 hours, as much as 80% of detail is lost.

The scale remains roughly the same regardless of the length of input time; thus a three-day course is fundamentally forgotten within a week to two weeks of completion.

The implications are disturbing; if a multi-national firm

spends $50 million per year on training, it can be shown that within a few days of that training's completion, if there is not appropriate reviewing programmed into the educational structure, $40 million has been lost with incredible efficiency.

By a simple understanding of the memory's rhythms, it is possible not only to avert this decline, but also to train personnel in such a way as to *increase* the amount learned in any training by using Additive Associative Techniques.

Your Brain Cell

In the last five years your brain cell has become the New Frontier in the human search for knowledge.

We have discovered that not only do we each have 1,000,000,000,000 brain cells, but that the interconnections between them can form patterns and memory traces that permute to a number so staggeringly large as to be functionally equivalent to infinite. The number, calculated by the Russian neuro-anatomist, Petr K. Anokhin, is one followed by ten million kilometres of standard 11pt typewritten noughts!

With this inherent capacity to integrate and juggle with the multiple billions of bits of data that each of us possess, it has become increasingly apparent to those in brain research that adequate training of our phenomenal biocomputer, which in one second can calculate what it would take the Cray computer, at 400 million calculations per second, 100 years to accomplish, will enormously accelerate and increase our ability to problem solve, to analyse, to prioritise, to create and to communicate.

Mental Abilities and Age

'They die!' is the usual chorus from people in response to the question: 'What happens to your brain cells as they get older?' It is usually voiced with an extraordinary and surprising enthusiasm.

One of the most delightful pieces of news from the brain research front comes from Dr. Marion Diamond of the University of California, who has recently confirmed that there is no evidence of brain cell loss with age in normal, active and healthy brains.

On the contrary, research is now indicating that if the brain is used and trained, there is a biological increase in the brain's interconnective complexity, i.e. intelligence is raised.

Training of people in their sixties, seventies, eighties and nineties has shown that in every area of mental performance statistically significant and permanent increases can be made with adequate training.

We are at the beginning of a revolution the like of which the world has never before seen: the Quantum-Leap in the development of human intelligence.

On the personal front, in education and in business, information from the psychological, neuro-physiological and educational laboratories is being used to rapidly dissolve problems which had hitherto been accepted as a normal part of the human condition.

By applying our knowledge of the brain's separate functions, by externally reflecting our internal processes in Mind Map form, by making use of the innate elements and rhythms of memory, and by applying our knowledge of the brain cell and the possibilities for continued improvement throughout life, we realise that the Intelligence War can indeed be won. The losers are no-one, the victors you and everyone.

Stop Your Timer Now

Length of time .... mins

SELF TEST 1 (1,900 words)

1. The top eighty per cent of British companies invest considerable money and time in training.   True False

2. Most, but not all, of the mental skill areas can, with the aid of modern research on the function of the brain, be tackled with relative ease.   True False

3. Number is a left cortex dominant function.   True False

4. Music is a left cortex dominant function.   True False

5. Imagination is a right cortex dominant function.   True   False

6. The right cortex is the 'creative' side.   True   False

7. The great artists, such as Cezanne, were right cortex dominant.   True   False

8. In Mind Maps, a key word is placed in the centre of the page in order to facilitate memorisation and the creative generation of ideas.   True   False

9. Using new super-speed reading techniques you can develop speeds of well over 1,000 words a minute.   True   False

10. Mnemonic techniques were originally invented by the Greeks, and are sound systems to help improve memory.   True   False

11. Human recall actually rises shortly after a learning period is completed.   True   False

12. Ninety per cent of detail is forgotten within twenty four hours.   True   False

13. In the average human brain, there are 1,000,000,000,000 brain cells.   True   False

14. The Cray computer is finally approaching the capacity of the brain in its overall ability to calculate.   True   False

15. Dr. Marion Diamond of the University of California has recently confirmed that only a few people lose brain cells as they get older.   True   False

Comprehension .... Right

Percentage ....

CHAPTER TWO

READING – A NEW DEFINITION

*Definition is the companion of Clarity; Clarity is
the guide to your goals.*

Think for a moment what reading is, and write your definition
in the space below:

Now compare your definition with common ones such as
'reading is understanding what the author intended', 'reading is taking in the written word', 'reading is the assimilation
of printed information'.

Each of these standard definitions takes in *a part* of the real
definition of reading, which must include the full range of
skills necessary throughout the process.

Reading may thus be defined as a seven-part process
comprised of the following steps:

1. *Recognition*
   The reader's knowledge of the alphabetic symbols. This
   step takes place almost before the physical aspect of
   reading begins.

2. *Assimilation*
   The physical process by which light is reflected from the
   word and is received by the eye, then transmitted via the
   optic nerve to the brain.

3. *Intra-integration*
   The equivalent to basic comprehension, and refers to the
   linking of all parts of the information being read with all
   other appropriate parts.

4. *Extra-integration*

This includes analysis, criticism, appreciation, selection and rejection. The process in which the reader brings the whole body of his previous knowledge to what he is reading, making the appropriate connections.

5. *Retention*

The basic storage of information. Storage can itself become a problem. Most readers will have experienced entering an examination room and storing most of their information during the two hour exam period! Storage, then, is not enough, and must be accompanied by recall.

6. *Recall*

The ability to get back out of storage that which is needed, preferably *when* it is needed.

7. *Communication*

The use to which the information is immediately or eventually put; includes the very important subdivision: thinking.

In the light of this definition, it can be seen that the common reading problems originally outlined in *Use Your Head:*

vision	fatigue	recall
speed	laziness	impatience
comprehension	boredom	vocabulary
time	interest	subvocalisation
amount	analysis	typography
surroundings	criticism	literary style
noting	motivation	selection
retention	appreciation	rejection
age	organisation	concentration
fear	regression	back-skipping

and the more general learning problems outlined in the Intelligence War, page 17, can all be dealt with easily by the reader who has learned to recognise the print and to assimilate, comprehend, understand, retain, recall and communicate.

In the next chapter, we shall deal specifically with some of the more major and specific common reading problem areas.

CHAPTER THREE

THE COMMON READING PROBLEMS – SUBVOCALISATION, FINGER-POINTING, REGRESSION AND BACK-SKIPPING – NEW APPROACHES TO OVERCOMING THEM

Once a problem is faced, analysed and understood, it becomes a positive energy centre for the creation of solutions.

In this chapter I shall deal with some of the problems most often mentioned and listed before, including subvocalisation, finger-pointing, regression, and back-skipping – areas that are major barriers to efficient reading. I shall include new approaches based on the most recent research on the functioning and relationship of the eye and brain to both solutions and explanations, correcting much of what has been written on these subjects.

Subvocalisation

A common major reading problem is 'subvocalisation', the tendency to 'mouth' the words you are reading. It is a product of the way in which children are taught to read: usually by the phonetic or phonic method or the look-say method.

The Phonic Method

Can you remember by which method you were taught? It was probably the phonic method, or the look-say method, or a combination of both.

The phonic method first introduces the child to the ordinary alphabet from a to z, and then introduces the various sounds of each letter so that 'a' can become 'ah', 'be' can become 'buh', and so on. The child is then introduced to the letters and sounds in the context of words. Thus 'the cat' will first be read 'tuh-heh-eh kuh-ah-tuh' (not see-aye-tee etc.) until the teacher has moulded the word into its proper form. When the child has learned to make the correct sounds (vocalises properly) he is told to read silently. This last stage often takes a long time, and many children and even adults never get past the stage of moving their lips while reading. Those who *do* get past this stage may nevertheless still be vocalising *to themselves*. That is to say, as they read, they are consciously aware of the sound of each word. This is *subvocalisation*.

The Look-Say Method
The look-say method of teaching children to read also relies on a word or verbal response. The child is shown a picture, for example a cow, with the word that represents the object printed clearly beneath it, thus: C O W. The teacher then asks the child for the correct response. If the incorrect answer is given (for example 'elephant'!) the teacher guides the child to the correct response and then moves on to the next word. It can be seen that when the child has reached a reasonable level of proficiency he will be in a position similar to the child who has been taught by the phonic method: able to read, still verbalising, and told that he should read silently.

These are of course only brief outlines, but they do help to illustrate that children who have completed their instruction in learning to read are left with the habit of vocally or subvocally repeating the words they are reading.

Virtually every book and course on speed reading maintains that this habit is one of the greatest barriers to improvement and that it *must* be overcome.

The truth of the matter is that you can benefit from subvocalisation. It does, undoubtedly, hold the reader back in certain circumstances, especially when he is dependent upon it for understanding, but this is not necessary. In the real sense of the word subvocalisation *cannot* and should not be completely eliminated. Once this is understood, the 'problem' may be approached in its proper perspective, leading to much more satisfactory reading habits. People who are instructed to 'eliminate subvocalisation' often become discouraged and lose enjoyment in reading altogether after attempting for weeks to accomplish the impossible.

The proper approach to this problem is to accept that while subvocalisation *always* persists, it can be pushed farther and farther back into the 'semi-conscious'. In other words, while never being able to eliminate the habit completely, you can become less dependent upon it. Bearing this approach in mind, you need not worry when you occasionally realise that you are subvocalising, because it is a universal habit. What you should try to do is to become less dependent on this habit for complete understanding.

A positive side to this habit is that you can actually use subvocalisation to *aid* the remembering of what has been read. Assuming that practice has enabled you to become less dependent on subvocalisation, you can consciously increase the 'volume' of subvocalisation when reading important words or concepts, thus making that bit of information stand out from the rest.

In addition to this, it will help you to realise that subvocalisation is not by definition a slow plodding process. It is quite possible for your brain to subvocalise as many as 2,000 words per minute. Indeed there are now actually a number of people who can *speak* at above 1,000 words per minute. So only start worrying, if it is your choice to worry, when you reach these speeds!

Finger-Pointing

Another area of great controversy is finger-pointing. Many authorities consider it to be an extremely bad habit. Teachers in infant schools are continually faced with children whose finger is planted firmly under the words they are learning to read. Children seem to feel that with their finger serving as a pointer they can more easily guide their eyes to the part of the page they wish to read.

Many teachers discourage this, however, insisting that the child take his finger *off* the page and 'read properly'. Why? The answer is not clear. I have asked a number of teachers (and teachers of teachers) and the answer usually given is that the finger 'slows the child down'. This may well be the case, if the child feels secure with his finger under a word and does not wish to move on to the *next* word. But it is not a valid reply. For surely if the finger is placed on the book by the child because it helps his eyes, and if the teacher feels that the actual placing of the finger slows the child down, then the answer is *not* to tell the child to take his finger *off* the page, but to tell him to speed it up.

If you happen to be a finger-pointer don't be perturbed – it is a natural habit and, if used properly, may lead to a great increase in reading efficiency. To begin with, you may find difficulty in speeding up your finger, because you will have become used to a certain rhythm and speed, but if you persevere solid gains are not too far away. In Chapter 6 you will learn advanced finger movement and eye-guiding techniques.

Regression and Back-Skipping
Regression and back-skipping are similar and distinct. The following distinction should help to place them in their proper perspective. *Regression* is a conscious returning to words, phrases or paragraphs you feel you have missed or misunderstood. Many readers feel they must return to them in order to understand the material. *Back-skipping* is a kind of visual tic, an unconscious skipping back to words or phrases that have just been read. You are almost never aware that you are back-skipping.

As outlined in Chapter 5 on eye movements, back-skipping and regression add to the number of eye fixations per line, slowing down the reading process. Both of these habits are usually unnecessary. Studies performed in the conscious re-reading of material indicate that readers who were *sure* they needed to return to certain words or sections for understanding showed little change in comprehension scores when not allowed to do so. It is not so much a matter of comprehension as of confidence in your mind's ability.

The approach to eliminating or reducing these two habits is two-fold: A. Initially you must *force* yourself not to re-read sections you think you may have missed. B. Then you must gradually push up your speed, trying to maintain an even rhythm in your eye movements. Both speed and rhythm will make back-skipping and regression more difficult, while actually improving your comprehension.

The three problem areas: subvocalisation, finger-pointing, and back-skipping and regression may now no longer be seen as the major barriers so many people have made them out to be. They are simply habits that can be adjusted, and in many cases used to great advantage.

You are now ready to take your second Self Test. Since taking the first test you have learnt about the various problems many people have with reading, and their solutions. In this next test put your new knowledge to work; try to increase the length of each fixation and try to overcome whatever problems you have been having. *Consciously* push yourself a bit faster than you would normally read, while making every effort to comprehend what you are reading. When you have finished this exercise calculate your w.p.m. as before (in this article there are 1,500 words), answer the questions that follow, calculate your comprehension and enter both scores on your progress graphs.

From this point on in most of your reading, push yourself to go just that *little bit* faster.

Start Your Timer Now

SELF TEST 2
INTRODUCTION TO PSYCHOLOGY

The Definition of Psychology

Psychology may be defined as *the science that studies the behaviour of man and other animals*. It is, in other words, the study of *you* and is one of the most exciting fields of study in modern science. In reading *Speed Reading* you are in fact studying practical psychology.

For this definition to be useful, it is necessary to specify more clearly what psychologists mean by behaviour. We can get some idea of what *behaviour* means to the psychologist if we look briefly at the topics covered by psychology:

1. *The behaving organism.* As a science rooted in biology, psychology is interested in the bodily processes that make activity possible. Thus psychologists often refer to the stimuli (singular stimulus) that impinge upon sense organs, and to the responses that occur because of the way the organism operates. Stimuli include the lights, sounds, odours, pin-pricks, and other physical energy sources that are the external (and sometimes internal) occasions for what the organism

does, goading it to action, interrupting what it is doing, directing its choices. The responses (in humans) are what they do when their brains are active, their muscles move, and their glands secrete. We therefore touch briefly on the operation of the *skeleton* and the *muscles*, moving on to glance at the varied functioning of the endocrine (ductless) glands, such as the thyroid or the sex glands. But psychologists are particularly interested in the *nervous system* and especially in the *central nervous system*, whose most complex portion is the *brain*.

It has been found, for example, that there are centres deep in the brain (in a part of the brain, old from an evolutionary standpoint, called the hypothalamus) that appear to produce the equivalent of pleasure or of pain when these centres are electrically stimulated (Olds and Olds, 1965). Psychologists not only participated in the original experiments in which this discovery was made, but have since carried out a number of further experiments to determine how similar the responses to electrical stimulation of the brain are to the effects of external pain or food reward. For example, studies have been made of the reaction to conflict when a thirsty rat receives an electric shock as it attempts to drink. The rat at once approaches the water and withdraws from it in fear, assuming a characteristic posture. When the shock is received through an implanted electrode in the brain, the rat behaves just as if a shock had been received on its snout. Thus it appears plausible that the shock through the electrode is equivalent to painful stimulation.

2. *Growth and development.* The child is indeed 'father of the man.' We can understand much of adult behaviour only through a knowledge of the course of its development in the child. Two principles stand out as we study human development. One is that the growth of the body and the nervous system follows certain patterns rooted in biology. These are reflected in the concept of *maturation* of the organism along built-in (inherited) lines. The other is that a mature organism is also a product of *learning*. In man, this learning is in part a product of *social living*, a product of his *culture*. Hence in studying human development, we are interested in the processes of socialization, that is, the ways in which the infant turns into a civilized person.

3. *Motivation and emotion.* The newborn infant is aroused to activity by his bodily needs – the needs for air, food, elimination, a comfortable temperature, sleep. All such needs are the physiological roots of what psychologists call motivation. But motives become complex as the individual grows up, and psychologists study how they are acquired, how strong they are, and how people differ in their motives. Some individuals conform readily to their cultures, others rebel; some develop good work habits and have high motives to achieve, others are more shiftless; some are competitive and aggressive, others self-effacing. Emotions and motives are closely related, for the excitement of highly motivated activity has its emotional colouring; aggressive behaviour may be accompanied by deep feelings of anger, flight from danger by strong fear.

4. *Perception.* We perceive the world through our eyes or ears or by way of our other senses. But what is perception? How is it that we recognize a given colour as red, or hear one sound as music and another as noise, or 'sense' that one facial expression is friendly and another hostile? From its earliest days psychology has devoted a great deal of attention to such questions. It is clear that perception depends not only on our equipment of sense organs, but also on the structures in our nervous system which enable us to say 'This is hot' or 'That tastes salty.'

We shall be concerned too with problems of consciousness. How does our physiological state when alert and awake differ from conditions of sleep? We shall see that there is no sharp distinction between conscious and unconscious states; rather there are degrees of awareness in which we may be more or less receptive to stimuli in the environment. Even during the stage of sleep where dreaming occurs we may be affected by events that take place around us.

5. *Learning and thinking.* Because of its importance learning is a topic of special interest to psychologists, both in its theoretical aspects and in its practical aspects. The theoretical problems of learning include the answers to such puzzling questions as how rewards and punishments operate; what goes on when we remember and when we forget, or when we acquire skills; how learning one thing affects the learning

of others. The answers to these questions have important practical consequences, for much social effort goes into learning and teaching – of the young by parents and teachers, of apprentices on the job, of members of industrial and business organizations as they face new tasks.

A new interest in 'programmed' learning, often using so-called teaching machines, illustrates the practical consequences of experimental studies of learning. *A programme* is an attempt to apply what we know about the essential features of learning to the task of individual instruction, using a technique in which each step of the process is carefully planned to provide the best conditions for learning. We shall consider later the detailed ways in which such programmes make use of learning theory; for the present we may merely indicate that there have been promising successes in their use. For example, it has been reported that elementary school children who studied their mathematics by using a programme presented by a computer-controlled teaching machine did much better than those who learned it in the conventional way (Suppes, 1967).

Thinking and problem-solving make use of what we have learned, and thereby provide the occasions for new learning. The interrelations between learning and thinking, including the role of language, furnish plenty of subjects for investigation.

6. *Individuality and personality.* Individual uniqueness is a product of the hereditary and environmental influences that have shaped the person; the accidents of his birth and upbringing, what he has perceived and learned, what he has thought about. Psychologists have developed various ways of assessing or measuring many kinds of differences among people. Perhaps the most familiar of these devices is the intelligence test.

But intelligence is only one aspect of individuality. All of us know people of whom we say 'He's a real person' (or, regrettably, 'He's got quite a personality'). What is personality? What is it that conclusively distinguishes one individual from another? And what do we mean when we speak of the 'self'? These are questions of much concern to psychologists.

7. *Conflict, adjustment, and mental health.* For many

readers, this aspect of psychology may seem the most important. How do people meet frustration and conflict? What happens when they can no longer cope with their problems in ordinary ways? Is 'Adjustment' an ideal, or not? What, indeed, is mental health? While psychology has no final answers to these questions, it has at least been able to shed some light on them. There have been some successes in applying the methods of the experimental laboratory to these fields, and much has been accomplished in developing new techniques for treating mentally ill individuals.

8. *Social aspects of psychology.* The old saying; 'Two's company and three's a crowd,' familiar as it may seem in one context, illustrates a number of basic psychological questions. What is the difference between the response of an individual to his physical environment and his response to that same environment in the presence of another individual? What do we mean by a group, and how does group behaviour differ from and affect individual behaviour?

Stop Your Timer Now

Length of time .... mins

SELF TEST 2 (1,500 words)

1. Psychology is the science devoted to the study of the behaviour of man only.   True False

2. The science of psychology is rooted in biology.   True False

3. The central nervous system is the most important part of the nervous system, and does not include the brain.   True False

4. We cannot understand much of adult behaviour through a knowledge of its development in the child.   True False

5. The two principles that stand out as we study human development are motivation and emotion.   True False

35

6. Bodily needs are the psychological roots of emotion.　　　　　　　　　　　　True　False

7. Emotions and motives are closely related.　　　True　False

8. Perception depends only on our sense organs.　　　　　　　　　　　　　　True　False

9. Psychology has recently been able to make a sharp distinction between conscious and unconscious states.　　　　　　　　True　False

10. The theoretical problems of learning include the answers to such questions as how rewards and punishments operate.　　True　False

11. Programmed learning makes use of integration but does not yet use teaching machines.　　　　　　　　　　　　True　False

12. Individual uniqueness is a product determined solely by heredity or genetic 'passing on'.　　　　　　　　　　　True　False

13. Intelligence is not really an aspect of individuality.　　　　　　　　　　True　False

14. Psychology has a number of final answers to the question of mental health.　　　　True　False

15. 'Two's company and three's a crowd' is quoted because it illustrates one basic psychological question.　　　　　True　False

Comprehension .... Right

Percentage ....

CHAPTER FOUR

IMPROVING YOUR CONCENTRATION AND INCREASING YOUR COMPREHENSION

The power of maintained concentration is claimed by many of the world's Great Brains to be the prime factor in their success. When you master this, your eye-brain system becomes laser-like in its ability to focus and absorb. Your capacity to do this is, according to researchers in the field, infinite.

Having tackled basic theory and basic problems, we are now ready to discuss the concepts of concentration and comprehension and the physical conditions in which they can be maximised.

Concentration is most important if you are to get full value from the material you are reading. If you yourself have not experienced difficulty in this area, I am sure you will have heard others complaining that they just could not 'settle down' to the reading task at hand. In many cases even when they really wanted to read something they found themselves unable to do so.

Why is Poor Concentration Often Considered the Major Reading Problem?

The many causes for lack of concentration include vocabulary difficulties; conceptual difficulty of the material; inappropriate speed; incorrect mental approach or set; poor organisation; lack of interest; and lack of motivation.

Following is a discussion of each major problem area and solutions to each problem:

1. Vocabulary Difficulties

The Problem

After having increased your vocabulary with the information and exercises in Chapters 14, 15 and 16 you will already be on the way to solving this one. In addition:

The Solution

If the material being read continually confronts you with words which you do not understand or understand only vaguely, concentration will gradually become worse, because the ideas you are trying to absorb will be interrupted by gaps in understanding. A smooth inflow of information, unhampered by the lurking fear of misunderstanding, is a necessity for efficient reading. The vocabulary analysis and exercises in this book are designed to overcome this difficulty.

If you come to a word that you do not understand, just underline it and read on. Usually the meaning becomes vaguely apparent from the context of the sentence. Then, at the end of the chapter or that day's reading, you can do a 'Dictionary Run' and look them *all* up.

2. Conceptual Difficulty of the Material

The Problem

This is a slightly more difficult problem to overcome and usually arises in study books.

The Solution

The best approach is to 'multiple read' the material using the information on the guide. Skimming, scanning, paragraph structure and previewing are discussed thoroughly in later chapters and in *Use your Head*.

3. Inappropriate Reading Speed

The Problem

This is often a product of the school system. When children are given important or difficult material, they are usually told: 'read this *slowly* and *carefully*'. This approach establishes a vicious circle, because the more slowly one reads the less one understands, which makes the material seem even more indigestible. Ultimately a point of complete frustration is reached and the material is often abandoned in despair.

The Solution
If you have difficulty with concentration and comprehension this may well be your trouble, so vary your speeds on problem material, trying to go faster rather than more slowly, and you may find a great improvement. By learning to Speed and Range read, you will have control and choice of the appropriate speed for the material, needs, time of day, energy level and internal and external environments.

4. Incorrect Mental Approach or Set

The Problem
This simply means that your mind has not really been directed in the best way toward the material you are trying to read. You may, for instance, still be concentrating on an argument that took place in the office, or a social engagement for the coming evening.

The Solution
What you must try to do is to 'shake out' the unnecessary threads that are running through your mind, directing yourself to think *actively* about the subject you are reading. You may even go so far as to stop for a moment and purposefully gather together your thoughts. One way to do this most efficiently is to do a rapid two-minute Mind Map (Chapter 11) on the topic you are studying in order to *re-collect* your thoughts and to provide you with an even stronger on-going mental set. We shall be examining the question of mental set in greater detail in Chapter 7.

5. Poor Organisation

The Problem
This is a far commoner sin than many realise. Actually getting down to reading a book is a problem of the will, and almost demands a run-up to the desk in order to gain enough impetus actually to sit down at it. Having arrived and started to read many people suddenly realise that they don't have a pencil,

note-paper, their glasses and any number of other things, and consequently disrupt their concentration to get these materials.

The Solution
The solution is easy: before you sit down to read, make sure that all the materials you will need are readily available (see Chapter 7).

6. Lack of Interest
The Problem
This is a problem most often experienced by students or people taking special courses. We devote special attention to it in our reading courses. The first step in correcting this problem is to review the items discussed in this chapter, for lack of interest is often related to other difficulties: obviously interest will be difficult to maintain if a deficient vocabulary is continually interrupting understanding, if the material is confusing, if other thoughts keep popping up, and if necessary materials are not available.

Assuming that these problems are overcome and that interest is still not as high as it should be, analyse your personal approach to the material.

The Solution
The first step is to make sure that the technique being used is appropriate, and here I once again refer you to the Mind Map Organic Study Technique (Chapter 17). If all this fails, the following approach has proved useful to those who have come to what they thought was 'the end of the line'. This approach makes you a *Severe Critic*. Rather than reading the material as you normally would, get annoyed at it for having presented you with problems and try to analyse it thoroughly, concentrating especially on the negative aspects. You will find yourself actually becoming interested in the material, much in the way you become interested in listening to the arguments of someone whom you don't particularly like and wish to oppose vigorously.

7. Lack of Motivation

The Problem
This is different problem, often stemming from having no clearly defined purpose.

The Solution
The solution follows the same approach as in solving the problem of lack of interest, but should this fail to work you must analyse your reasons for reading the book or article in the first place. Often such a close look will lead to realisations that were previously dormant and increase motivation and desire. Sometimes this close look will lead you to the conclusion that you need not read the book at all. If the reasons in this respect are valid then, indeed, there is no point in reading the book. I must warn here that this may become a habit for those few who like to take the easy way out – so beware! Also affecting concentration and thereby comprehension is the influence, positive or negative, exerted by the external and internal environments. To create these to best effect, see Chapter 7.

Now, with some basic information about the brain, a new definition of reading, new ways of handling the major reading problem areas, and an increased ability to concentrate and comprehend, we will take you on a journey to explore one of the most incredible objects in the known universe: your own eye!

PART TWO

YOUR AMAZING EYES

Your eyes are one of the wonders of the Universe! At the back of each eye, in an area no larger than a thumbnail, are contained 130 million light receivers. All together these retinal light receivers receive and decode hundreds of photons (light bundles of energy) per second.

Acting in harmony, these light receivers can decode, in *less than a second*, a scene containing *billions* of bits of information with supra-photographic accuracy.

'Eyes' at the Back of Your Head
The phenomenally complex images decoded by your retinal light receivers are sent along a giant nerve, the Optic Nerve, and transmitted to the visual area of your brain – the Occipital Lobe. The Occipital Lobe is, paradoxically, not situated just behind the eyes, but is situated at the *back of your head!* Thus if anyone attempts to insult you by saying you are 'talking out of the back of your head', you can thank them for complimenting you on being a visual individual!

Pupil Size – Variations
We have known for some time that pupil size adjusts according to light intensity and nearness. The brighter the light and the nearer the object, the smaller will the pupil size be.

Western scientists have recently discovered that pupil size also varies with emotion, and that if you are confronted with a sight that especially interests you (like a member of the opposite sex) your pupil size will automatically increase. Such changes are small, but can be noticed by careful observation. Jade dealers in China have been aware of it for many years. While presenting objects for the customer's inspection, the dealer pays particularly close attention to the customer's eyes, waiting for an increase in pupil size. When this increase has been observed, the dealer knows that the customer is 'hooked' and sets an appropriate price.

Knowing these amazing new facts about the eyes, it becomes clear that traditional reading habits and reading speeds *must* be a product of mis-training and misuse; that if they were understood and trained properly, their functions would significantly improve.

This is indeed the case, and in the next chapter you will learn how to control and use these remarkable instruments.

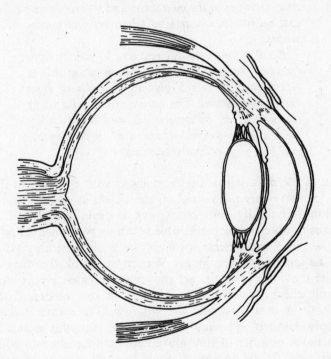

Fig. 2   Cross-section of the human eye

CHAPTER FIVE

GAINING CONTROL OF YOUR EYE MOVEMENTS TO INCREASE YOUR SPEED AND COMPREHENSION

Each of your eyes is the most amazing optical instrument known to Mankind, dwarfing by comparison even the most advanced macrocosmos- and microcosmos-searching telescopes and microscopes.

Each of your retinas contains 130 million light receivers, each of these 130 million being able to receive and process 5 photons (bundles of light energy) per second. The nature of this miraculous instrument can be understood, and being understood can be controlled and used to your extraordinary advantage.

One of the most surprising facts about your eyes is that they see properly *only when fixed* on the object at which they are looking. (Actually your seeing eye is never *entirely* still. It makes minute and imperceptible scanning movements known as 'saccadic' movements, probably to avoid an image falling on the same nerve receptors). We tend to think that they see while moving, when in fact movement creates a blur. As a simple check, watch people in trains or any moving vehicle looking at things outside the window. Their eyes will not simply 'absorb' all that passes by – you will notice an enormous number of tiny movements taking place in which their eyes 'fix' on an object, move to another and 'fix' on an object, move to another and 'fix' on that, and so on.

It is the same with reading. Most people, when asked to describe how their eyes move during the reading process, are likely to say that they glide smoothly over each line, pausing briefly at the end before going back to the beginning of the next. It seems to be a continuous and flowing movement, although many people will admit that their eyes go back over certain words.

In fact the reading process is quite different, and the eye, as it does when seeing anything clearly, takes in the printed information only when it is still. You may well ask 'how can we possibly read at all if the eye takes in the words only when it is still?'

The answer is that the eyes make small and fairly regular 'jumps'. These take the eye from fixation point to fixation point, usually a bit more than a word at a time.

To sum up, the eye does *not* move smoothly over the page at all, but instead moves in small jerks from left to right, pausing momentarily to take in a word or two before moving on and repeating the process. This can be clearly explained by the use of a diagram.

Fig. 3   Diagram of the eyes' progression while reading

While the eye is moving and pausing, moving and pausing in this way, the information is absorbed, as has been explained, *only during the pauses*. These pauses take up most of the time, and as each pause may last from one-quarter to one-and-a-half seconds, it can be seen that an improvement in reading speed is indeed possible by spending less time on each pause.

Before going on with this, let us look at the diagram on page 46 of the eye movements of a very poor reader.

This reader makes about twice as many pauses, or *fixations* as they are commonly called, as are required for good comprehension. His extra pauses are caused by the fact that he often re-reads words, sometimes skipping back as many as three places to make sure that he has taken in the correct meaning. These habits of back-skipping (returning, almost as a habit, to words that have just been read) and regression (returning

BACK-SKIPPING OR REGRESSION

WORD

Fig. 4   Diagram of a poor reader's eye movements

consciously to words which the reader feels he has missed or misunderstood) cause the poor reader's excessive number of fixations as shown in Fig. 4. On a simple mathematical basis, i.e. the addition of the time that he takes for each pause, his reading rate must inevitably be slower.

Now, what about the good reader? Let us diagram his eye movements first and then discuss them, while explaining at the same time how the poor reader can go about improving his own efficiency by eliminating certain bad habits and practising more efficient ones:

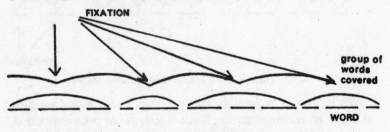

FIXATION

group of words covered

WORD

Fig. 5   Diagram of a good reader's eye movements

We immediately see from this diagram that the good reader, while not back-skipping or regressing, has also lengthened his 'jumps'. He no longer takes in a word or a little more at a time but has progressed to being able to take in two or three words at one fixation. If we assume for the moment that each fixation takes the same time, and set that time arbitrarily at ½ second, we can see that his total reading time for eight words is ½ + ½ + ½ + ½ = two seconds, whereas the poor reader, for the same line, takes ½ + ½ + ½ + ½ + ½ + ½ + ½ + ½ + ½ + ½ + ½ + ½ + ½ + ½ + ½ + ½ = eight seconds, or four times as long.

46

Your first task, then, is to work at eliminating these bad habits. Since widening the awareness of the visual span helps eliminate back-skipping and regression, we shall start with that.

The exercises that follow are designed to make you more aware of your own visual span, and will provide motivation for taking in more at a glance as you read. Use a card to cover up the numbers. Expose each number as *briefly as possible*, giving yourself no more than a split second to see it. Almost at the same time as it is uncovered it should be recovered.

Then write in the space next to the number what you think that number is, and check yourself to see whether you were right or wrong. Continue to the next number, from column to column, repeating the process until the page has been completed. You will find that the exercise becomes more difficult as you progress, because the number of digits is gradually increased. If you can reach the end of the six-digit numbers without having made any mistakes you will have done extremely well.

You will find that with practice you will be able to complete the six digit numbers in one flash, and this will give you increased confidence to take in two or more words at a time as you read. The numbers that follow include just enough examples of each digit-grouping to allow your eye/brain to practise and get accustomed to each level before moving you on to the next.

25	....	52	....
73	....	78	....
81	....	62	....
90	....	72	....
21	....	52	....
34	....	28	....
65	....	23	....
24	....	30	....
45	....	01	....
12	....	84	....
71	....	42	....

19	....	66	....
49	....	75	....
22	....	05	....
39	....	27	....
95	....	87	....
76	....	83	....
44	....	14	....
20	....	59	....
82	....	48	....
98	....	77	....
57	....	86	....
17	....	02	....
276	....	863	....
832	....	824	....
012	....	952	....
735	....	424	....
225	....	735	....
128	....	489	....
902	....	362	....
270	....	645	....
735	....	725	....
725	....	724	....
875	....	324	....
012	....	634	....
776	....	727	....
227	....	728	....
534	....	752	....
644	....	234	....
189	....	721	....
706	....	853	....
620	....	825	....
525	....	214	....

160	....		711	....
641	....		862	....
394	....		875	....
552	....		112	....
962	....		829	....
629	....		926	....
662	....		929	....
262	....		296	....
723	....		825	....
237	....		258	....
327	....		582	....
727	....		828	....
766	....		765	....
544	....		165	....
112	....		865	....
751	....		755	....
678	....		753	....
552	....		102	....
012	....		214	....
521	....		014	....
340	....		860	....
803	....		410	....
412	....		360	....
907	....		057	....
861	....		863	....
831	....		955	....
863	....		524	....
864	....		736	....
836	....		634	....
746	....		736	....
108	....		106	....
250	....		746	....

981	....		836	....
824	....		214	....
210	....		846	....
266	....		879	....
836	....		625	....
107	....		102	....
410	....		216	....
715	....		869	....
975	....		543	....
778	....		655	....
743	....		457	....
764	....		167	....
215	....		561	....
076	....		640	....
864	....		654	....
876	....		667	....
754	....		301	....
865	....		109	....
198	....		616	....
8636	....		7474	....
7874	....		7355	....
1177	....		1087	....
2276	....		2435	....
7425	....		8655	....
7654	....		6422	....
7776	....		6554	....
5432	....		6544	....
7656	....		5432	....
9879	....		8701	....
8611	....		0187	....
9870	....		0676	....

8765	....	3342	....
3776	....	2243	....
7543	....	7701	....
1073	....	7653	....
7653	....	7622	....
8763	....	5432	....
5324	....	6542	....
6422	....	7055	....
0652	....	8764	....
8643	....	7654	....
6117	....	1153	....
7702	....	8673	....
5422	....	7533	....
8761	....	5733	....
8276	....	7373	....
7271	....	8861	....
0176	....	1760	....
8766	....	2344	....
7653	....	5432	....
6510	....	6530	....
1074	....	7119	....
9840	....	1105	....
7531	....	7401	....
8376	....	8764	....
1876	....	2876	....
1652	....	7654	....
1088	....	7601	....
6707	....	8754	....
8761	....	8110	....
3051	....	8765	....
2432	....	5492	....

7532	....	3346	....
6501	....	5443	....
8765	....	4455	....
7651	....	1877	....
1086	....	7550	....
8766	....	4466	....
8770	....	7701	....
8761	....	5420	....
1106	....	6243	....
4323	....	6421	....
9230	....	4429	....
5863	....	3327	....
6543	....	8761	....
9254	....	0185	....
1074	....	8242	....
7231	....	5530	....
1875	....	9872	....
9116	....	7049	....
5254	....	7285	....
2127	....	0423	....
4962	....	4671	....
6630	....	9014	....
7351	....	4185	....
3752	....	2753	....
8296	....	1172	....
9274	....	4827	....
5701	....	8566	....
3088	....	9862	....
2849	....	8421	....
76541	....	46532	....
75251	....	64321	....

19865	....	98010	....
44903	....	66254	....
37620	....	65432	....
95411	....	27548	....
95338	....	86421	....
15154	....	08435	....
85368	....	18642	....
36437	....	74322	....
47720	....	52740	....
76200	....	79284	....
51914	....	29476	....
68223	....	13654	....
01677	....	29370	....
82101	....	35726	....
44626	....	64651	....
50663	....	45609	....
27391	....	82546	....
99265	....	21419	....
56438	....	47538	....
14732	....	49762	....
38656	....	95078	....
63643	....	91636	....
30079	....	26090	....
17532	....	14160	....
98732	....	88572	....
17643	....	55621	....
49289	....	38247	....
79232	....	19376	....
82448	....	01753	....
28299	....	46517	....
57033	....	29645	....

49221	....	85321	....
70165	....	38585	....
93754	....	01763	....
01532	....	37479	....
92750	....	45072	....
62990	....	82643	....
15719	....	73152	....
93761	....	21814	....
07626	....	48211	....
50079	....	73760	....
49386	....	83742	....
94703	....	15228	....
95750	....	37542	....
17740	....	94666	....
28252	....	95470	....
48659	....	35438	....
94552	....	65221	....
01753	....	14702	....
72034	....	93225	....
83371	....	46013	....
83608	....	93972	....
26441	....	13286	....
48512	....	92035	....
95206	....	02561	....
84351	....	78246	....
16842	....	08221	....
93866	....	49652	....
84610	....	42982	....
12547	....	60257	....
62938	....	46103	....
47249	....	50251	....

52951	....	83703	....
07649	....	15732	....
29331	....	62968	....
345782	....	987103	....
201895	....	916845	....
456781	....	376519	....
569831	....	238754	....
387512	....	452875	....
984763	....	045017	....
298435	....	112784	....
090768	....	234742	....
954136	....	564219	....
759483	....	887631	....
656891	....	876925	....
332557	....	031409	....
476830	....	517194	....
219574	....	376489	....
857392	....	438752	....
386279	....	875315	....
619473	....	219563	....
219574	....	376981	....
487614	....	085376	....
764972	....	387519	....
114873	....	978563	....
576329	....	103865	....
657893	....	984371	....
349714	....	769102	....
496510	....	041672	....
392587	....	643191	....
567681	....	638725	....
284190	....	116793	....

767935	....	436794	....
432614	....	998664	....
816154	....	654731	....
764129	....	284937	....
084502	....	563981	....
278401	....	876943	....
801018	....	932547	....
342987	....	478901	....
865013	....	543789	....
987654	....	037685	....
765839	....	258764	....
965410	....	423698	....
356793	....	175893	....
763296	....	538721	....
090807	....	443244	....
578391	....	121376	....
578342	....	987531	....
013676	....	467831	....
284679	....	538762	....
998576	....	105789	....
334876	....	857643	....
876652	....	664892	....
189567	....	356542	....
987563	....	467557	....
958746	....	465378	....
836752	....	556793	....
001578	....	567832	....
378695	....	189695	....
276459	....	354672	....
287654	....	801567	....
765843	....	968476	....

CHAPTER SIX

GUIDING THE EYES – A NEW SPEED AND RANGE READING TECHNIQUE

*In the mental arena, it is often the first step that
is the most difficult. Successive steps become
successively more easy. Each advance is a greater
advance than the previous advance. The more you
learn the more easy it is for you to learn more.*

Up to this point I have dealt with traditional reading problems
and approaches, shedding where possible new light on these
areas. These and other Advanced Reading Techniques are
being taught by Buzan Centres around the world.

In this chapter you will be introduced to the full subject of
Speed and Range Reading. Some of the fundamental principles will be explained and you will start on the first steps to
these Advanced Methods. Using these *basic* hints, many of you
will notice considerable improvement in your already improved speed.

The underlying concept of the Advanced Techniques is that
the visual field (the area of space we normally see) can be used
more effectively in the reading process. You will remember
that in Chapter 5 I explained that your focus could be
stretched *along* the line in order to take in more words at a
glance. Advanced Reading proponents, and I am one of them,
see no reason why a reader cannot make use of his *vertical*
vision as well while reading. After all, when we look at
peoples' faces we do not look 'along a line'; we see an area
which we fully absorb. Why not do the same with print?

I have diagrammed in Fig. 6 the field of vision, showing the
various steps in the development of this more inclusive
focusing ability.

It is possible for us here to begin to develop a complete
Advanced Reading Technique.

The first step, and this may surprise you, is to use your

hand as a guide. Circle the thumb and forefinger of your hand, extend the other three fingers into a straight wedge, and with the palm upwards place your hand at an angle of 45° on the page. Commencing at the first line, smoothly sweep the tip of the wedge along that line, lift your hand about a ¼″ off the page and go back to the beginning of the next line where once again your finger-nails should just touch the page. Repeat this movement along the next line, get to the end, lift off the page, return, and so on.

It is important in this first stage to make sure that the movement is continuous and smooth, with no pauses or jerks at the end or beginning of lines.

Once you have mastered this movement, keeping your wrist, elbow and shoulder very relaxed, gradually speed up until your hand is going as fast as possible, and you have lost *all* comprehension. Repeat this exercise a number of times, and then go back for a normal reading moving the hand underneath the lines at a comfortable pace. Within a few days many of you will have doubled your already improved speeds.

When you have become accustomed to reading with the hand, try experimenting with a pen or pencil, similarly guiding them along underneath the line you are reading. Practice different angles, hand positions and styles with this, as each person tends to develop a personal technique after a couple of weeks of practice.

The eventual advantage of the pen or pencil is that, if held properly, they block less print, allowing the peripheral vision of your eyes to get 'sneak previews' of what is coming ahead, which allows your mind to prepare better for the material upon which your eyes will soon be focusing.

When you have achieved facility with this step, and when

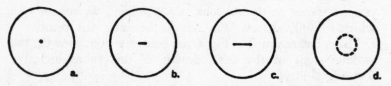

Fig. 6 a. Focus on a single letter, as when a child first learns to read by the phonic method. b. Focus on a single word (the poor-to-average reader). c. Focus on 4–5 words at a time (the good reader). Focus on groups or bunches of words (the Advanced Reader)

you have become accustomed to the major elements within it, you will be ready to try the next leap forward, which is to make use of a wide area of focus, as mentioned earlier. The exercise is similar to the one you have just completed, but instead of sweeping your hand under only one line, you sweep it under *two at a time*. This may feel very uncomfortable and prove difficult at first, as you are using entirely new visual techniques, but as usual perseverance will bring its reward.

I have diagrammed below the hand position to be used, and the movement it should make. You may use either hand.

Practice these guiding techniques on everything you read for the next few weeks, especially using a pencil, pen or thin, pointed object, as these are easy to use and give you constant accelerations in speed, while keeping the mind focused and its concentration consequently high.

In the initial stages the guide may seem to 'get in the way' but this difficulty is rapidly overcome, and the new habit quickly and beneficially established.

Later, in Chapter 9 you will find further exercises to increase your vertical as well as horizontal speeds.

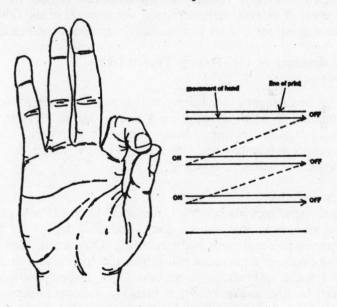

Fig. 7   Hand position – guiding technique

CHAPTER SEVEN

EYE-DEAL EXTERNAL AND INTERNAL ENVIRONMENTAL RANGE READING CONDITIONS

A positive internal environment will interact synergistically (1+1=2,3,5 →) with a positive external environment to create even more positive. A negative internal environment will similarly react synergistically with a negative external environment to create even more negative.

It is essential, if you are to remain literate, to understand this principle, and to apply the first of the two formulas.

Many times our concentration and comprehension are distracted and poor because of interruptions caused by our internal or external environments. Being aware of the following suggestions will let you create the optimum conditions.

1. Reading at the Wrong Time of Day

The Problem

This often makes the difference between a complete understanding of what is being read and a complete failure to understand it. Because of habits formed in school many have never experimented with the time of day at which they do their best reading or learning.

The Solution

Such experimentation is vital, for we all have different peaks and slumps in this regard. Some find that they study best between five and nine in the morning. Others find they can study only at night, and still others that periods in the late morning or early afternoon are best. If you suspect that timing may be the cause of your inability to concentrate and comprehend, experiment as soon as possible.

2. Poor Health

The Problem
This is an obvious drawback to any sustained efficient mental activity.

The Solution
If you are likely to be involved in an extensive reading or studying programme, you should do everything possible to make sure that your physical resources are adequate to the task. Even such minor illnesses as colds and headaches will make a difference to intellectual performance. If you have such symptoms semi-chronically, ask your doctor for advice. It is particularly useful, in conjunction with the advice, to start a gentle and consistent exercise programme.

3. Interference

The Problem
This may reach the point of infuriation, although some people welcome interference as an excuse to leave the task! Just as unknown words and difficult concepts break the flow of concentration and understanding, so do telephone calls, unnecessary breaks, loud noises, and lesser diversions like transistor radios, doodle-pads and other items of fidgety interest that often litter a desk, and your air space.

The Solution
The rule here is to make your studying environment sacro-sanct, and to arrange it so that it supports you. Little things such as putting the phone on an answering service, having a humorous sign on the door requesting peace; selecting appropriate music, and getting rid of unnecessary distractions, will all help you to become strong-minded. For more information on the environment, see page 63.

4. Physical Conditions

The Problem
These include:
(a) placement and intensity of light,

(b) height of chair and desk,
(c) distance of eyes from the reading material,
(d) availability of materials,
(e) physical comfort,
(f) environment.

The Solution

(a) Placement and Intensity of Light

The best light to study under is daylight, and where possible the desk or reading platform should be placed near a window. If this is not possible, and in times of the day when daylight is insufficient, light should come over the shoulder opposite to the hand with which you write, to avoid glare. Desk lamps can cause eye strain if not placed properly. The intensity of the light should be such as to illuminate adequately the material being read, and should not be too bright so as to form a great contrast with the rest of the room. The person who huddles up to his bright light lamp which beams directly on his book should take note. In addition to the desk lamp, it is well to have balanced general illumination.

(b) Height of Chair and Desk

The height of both chair and desk are important: the chair should be preferably straight-backed, and the height of chair should allow thighs to be parallel with floor or slightly raised from parallel in order to allow the main pressure for seating to be taken by the main sitting bones. Sometimes a small stool or phone directory can help to raise the feet to a comfortable level. A common desk height is 29–32″.

(c) Distance of the Eyes from the Reading Material

The distance of the eyes from the reading material should be approximately 18″, a natural distance if one sits properly as described. Keeping the reading material this far away makes it much easier for the eyes to focus on groups of words, and considerably lessens eye strain and the possibility of headaches from reading. To convince yourself of this, try looking at your forefinger when it is almost touching your nose and then look at your whole hand when it is about 18″ away from you. You will notice a real physical strain in the former, and a considerable easing of that strain in the latter even though you are 'taking in' more.

(d) Availability of Materials

We have already discussed the availability of materials and will add only that a properly organised desk is not only better for concentration and understanding, but can be also a psychological boost. Knowing that things are pleasingly and functionally placed increases the enjoyment and ease of the task at hand.

(e) Physical Comfort

Do not make yourself *too* comfortable! Many people look for the most comfortable and inviting easy-chair in the house, pad it even further with soft cushions, place a footrest in front of it so that they can stretch out more comfortably, prepare a hot drink or open a couple of cans of beer, and then settle down for two hours of intensive work to find two hours later that they have been adrift throughout!

Ideally your chair should be neither too hard nor too soft, should have a straight back-rest (a sloping one causes bad posture and back-strain and makes proper note-taking uncomfortable) and should in general neither make you too relaxed nor too tense.

(f) Environment

The environment in which you read and study will have an overall effect on your range of achievements. The place in which you read should be light, spacious, pleasing to your eye, touch and physical body, effectively organised for the reading purposes at hand, decorated to your taste, and a place to which you would want to go, even should you not be needing to read. Don't make it a punishment area or a prison cell!

Recollect how you feel inside (internal environment) when a special friend greets you warmly and invites you into a delightfully prepared room (external environment). That is the feeling you need to create for and in yourself as you think about the place where you go to read or study. It should invite and welcome you.

The Plus One Rule

The Plus One Rule is simply the following: every time you are consciously attempting to read faster, give yourself the goal of a minimum of one word per minute faster than you read at your previous highest speed. In this way you do not put unnecessary stress on yourself, and will often find that you have increased by ten or more words per minute, thus comfortably beating your goal, which leads to increasing confidence as well as faster and more efficient reading.

During the Self Test that follows, and the subsequent Self Tests in the book, give yourself a Ten-Plus rule, in which your goal is to increase by ten words per minute in each Self Test.

Start Your Timer Now

SELF TEST 3

THE METHODS OF SCIENCE

Observation and Experiment

The methods used by working scientists have evolved from a separation of methods used in ordinary life, particularly in the manual trades. First you have a look at the job and then you try something and see if it will work. In more learned language, we begin with observations and follow with *experiments*. Now everyone, whether he is a scientist or not, observes; but the important things are what to observe and how to observe them. In this sense the scientist and the artist are similar. The artist observes in order to analyse and record, through experience and observation, what is seen into some new and *integrated creation*. The scientist similarly observes in order to find things and relations that are as far as possible dependent on objective criteria. As Leonardo da Vinci said: 'Study the science of art and the art of science.' This does not mean that we should have no conscious aim. Far from it: as the history of science shows, some objective, often a practical one, is an essential requirement for the discovery of new things.

Classification and Measurement

Two techniques have in time grown out of naive observation: *classification and measurement*. Both are, of course, much older than conscious science, but they are now used in quite a special way. Classification has become in itself the first step towards understanding new groups of phenomena. They have to be put in order before anything can be done with them. Measurement is only one further stage of that putting in order. Counting is the ordering of one collection against another; in the last resort against the fingers. Measuring is counting the number of a standard collection that balance or line up with the quantity that is to be weighed or measured. It is measurement that links science with mathematics on the one hand, and with commercial and mechanical practice on the other. It is by measurement that numbers and forms enter science, and it is also by measurement that it is possible to indicate precisely what has to be done to reproduce given conditions and obtain a desired result.

It is here that the active aspect of science comes into the picture – that characterized by the word 'experiment'. After all, as the word indicates, it is only a trial, and early experiments indeed were full scale trials. Once measurement was introduced it was possible not only to reproduce trials accurately, but also to take the somewhat daring step of carrying them out on a small scale. It is that small-scale or model experiment that is the essential feature of modern science. By working on a small scale far more trials can be carried out at the same time and far more cheaply. Moreover, by the use of mathematics, far more valuable results can be obtained from the many small-scale experiments than from one or two elaborate and costly full scale trials.

All experiments boil down to two very simple operations: taking apart and putting together again; or in scientific language, analysis and synthesis. Unless you can take a thing or process to bits you can do nothing with it but observe it as an undivided whole. Unless you can put the pieces together again and make the whole thing work there is no way of knowing whether you have introduced something new or left something out in your analysis.

Apparatus

In order to carry out these operations, scientists have, over the course of centuries, evolved a complete set of material tools of their own – the *apparatus* of science. Apparatus is not anything mysterious. It is simply the tools of ordinary life turned to very special purposes. The crucible is just a pot, the forceps a pair of tongs. In turn, the apparatus of the scientist often comes back into practical life in the form of useful instruments or implements. It is not very long, for instance, since the modern television set was the cathode-ray tube, a purely scientific piece of apparatus devised to measure the mass of the electron. Scientific apparatus fulfils either of two major functions: as scientific instruments such as telescopes or microscopes, it can be used to extend and make more precise our sensory perception of the world; as scientific tools, such as micro-manipulators, stills, or incubators, it can be used to extend our motor manipulation of the things around us.

Laws, Hypotheses, and Theories

From the results of experiments, or rather from the mixture of operation and observation that constitutes experiments, comes the whole body of scientific knowledge. But that body is not simply a list of such results. If it were, science would soon become as unwieldy and as difficult to understand as the Nature from which it started. Before these results can be of any use, and in many cases before they can even be obtained, it is necessary to tie them together, so to speak, in bundles, to group them and to relate them to each other, and this is the function of the logical part of science. The arguments of science, the use of mathematical symbols and formulae, in earlier stages merely the use of names, lead to the continuous creation of the more or less coherent edifice of scientific *laws, principles, hypotheses, and theories*. And that is not the end; it is here that science is continually beginning, for, arising from such hypotheses and theories, there come the practical *applications* of science. These in turn, if they work, and even more often if they do not, give rise to new observations, new experiments, and new theories. Experiment, interpretation, application, all march on together and between them make up the effective, live, and social body of science.

The Language of Science

In the process of observation, experiment, and logical interpretation, there has grown up the *language* or rather, the languages, of science that have become in the course of time as essential to it as the material apparatus. Like the apparatus, these languages are not intrinsically strange; they derive from common usage and often come back to it again. A cycle was once *kuklos*, a wheel, but it lived many centuries as an abstract term for recurring phenomena before it came back to earth as a bicycle. The enormous convenience of making use of quite ordinary words in the forgotten languages of Greece and Rome was to avoid confusion with common meanings. The Greek scientists were under the great disadvantage of not having a word – in Greek – for it. They had to express themselves in a roundabout way in plain language – to talk about the submaxillary gland as 'the acorn-like lumps under the jaw'. But these practices, though they helped the scientists to discuss more clearly and briefly, had the disadvantage of building up a series of special languages or jargons that effectively, and sometimes deliberately, kept science away from the ordinary man. This barrier, however, is by no means necessary. Scientific language is too useful to unlearn, but it can and will infiltrate into common speech once scientific ideas become as familiar adjuncts of everyday life as scientific gadgets.

Stop Your Timer Now

Length of time .... mins

The section that you have just read contained 1,250 words. In order to calculate your words per minute, divide the number of minutes taken to read the article into the number of words. When you have done this, enter the wpm score in your progress graph on page 14.

Following are fifteen true or false questions. Circle the word next to the answer you think is correct, and when you have completed all fifteen check your answers with the answers on page 183. In order to keep your graphs visually distinct, enter your comprehension score, using a different coloured pen or pencil, in the same column as you have entered your reading score.

SELF TEST 3 (1,250 words)

1. Scientific methods were largely based on the observation of manual trades.   True False

2. The scientist observes and uses his own sentiments in order to find relationships.   True False

3. Subjective interpretation has become in itself the first step toward understanding new groups of phenomena.   True False

4. Science and mathematics are linked by order, not by measurement.   True False

5. Early experiments were done as full-scale trials.   True False

6. The small-scale experiment is the essential feature of modern science.   True False

7. All experiments boil down to three simple operations.   True False

8. The one basis for all experiments is synthesis.   True False

9. Scientific apparatus is derived from and is based upon the needs of science.   True False

10. The body of scientific knowledge is the product of operation and observation.   True False

11. Scientific laws and theories are claimed to be the end or goal of science.   True False

12. Scientific hypotheses but not the applications of science, give rise to new observations and experiments.   True False

13. The language of science derives from common usage.   True False

68

14. The word 'kuklos' has been applied to
non-recurring phenomena.   True False

15. Scientific language has kept science away
from the ordinary man.   True False

Comprehension .... Right

Percentage ....

CHAPTER EIGHT

DEVELOPING ADVANCED SKIMMING AND SCANNING SKILLS

Theoretically, the human visual system can photograph an entire page of print in one-twentieth of a second, and thus a standard length book in between six and twenty-five seconds, and the entire Encyclopaedia Britannica in less than an hour. Advanced skimming and scanning skills take you on the first step of that incredible and inevitable journey.

With the introduction of skimming and scanning we come to yet another area where there seems to be a considerable amount of misunderstanding and misdirected debate. In order to clarify this situation I shall first define the two concepts, and shall then discuss the various confusions. At the end of the chapter are exercises which will help not only to explain the concept of scanning but which will improve your scanning facility.

Skimming can be defined as that process in which your eye covers certain preselected sections of the material in order to gain a *general overview* of that material. In scanning your eye glances over material in order to find a *particular* piece of information.

Skimming is a more involved concept than scanning and is similar to the previewing techniques that I shall be discussing in later chapters. Its basic aim is to provide a skeleton on which the meat of the material can subsequently be placed. We shall be delving into the application of this process shortly.

Scanning is a more simple process that is usually applied when one is looking up a word in a dictionary, a name or telephone number in the directory, or a particular piece of information in a text book or report. The application of this concept is simple. All you have to do is to make sure before you scan that you know the basic lay-out of the material you are scanning. This enables you to save the time that so many people spend hunting around in the wrong sections for the information they desire.

It is possible, once you have mastered these skills of skimming and scanning, to develop them further in order to enable your eye to take in large areas of print at one time. This combines the more specialised skills of skimming and scanning with a *full* reading and comprehension skill. In Chapter 9, after you have completed more basic scanning exercises, you will be introduced to new techniques that will show you how to take in large areas of print at one time.

Can skimming, as some authors have claimed, be equated with reading, and vice-versa? My answer is a definite no! As I have already explained, skimming is simply selecting *parts* of the material to be read in order to gain an overview: the eye reads special little sections. This can in no way be considered to be reading the entire text.

Advanced reading schools like the Buzan Centres teach, under instructor supervision, methods of reading that enable the eye to take in large areas of print at one time while using some form of visual aid. *This* process can be defined as *reading* because the reader is taking in all the words on the page. It has been mistaken by many people to be simply a different form of skimming, whereas in fact it is a different form of reading.

The confusion arises from the fact that certain skimmers have refined their art to such an extent that their comprehension seems to indicate that they have indeed read all of the material, whereas in fact they have very cleverly selected the major points.

The situation is further confused by those who say that Advanced Reading methods using large areas of print are actually teaching people only to skim. This again is not the case, as both the physics of the eye movement and the approach to the information being absorbed are quite different in the separate cases.

On the pages that follow are a series of number-scanning exercises. Each page contains rows of numbers. The first number in each row is repeated *somewhere* across that row, and it is your task to spot it as quickly as possible. Start timing yourself, and with a pencil in one hand quickly check off the number in the row which corresponds to the number in the left hand column. When you have done this, record your time at the bottom of the page.

The exercises get more difficult as they progress, because the numbers are increased in size and are also made more similar. By training, you will be expanding the visual range of your 'mind's eye' thus allowing you to develop both your skimming and scanning abilities.

You may do these exercises in small 'bites' or all at once if you wish. It is important when you do them that you be as mentally alert as possible, so make sure your eyes are 'fresh' and that you are highly motivated.

27	92	73	27	56	28	38	76
45	76	87	45	32	85	40	83
37	86	84	59	37	63	27	41
51	84	32	67	85	93	51	43
58	65	32	74	38	58	91	57
62	54	27	69	62	34	21	95
76	63	76	53	27	31	62	54
95	67	43	26	95	61	50	53
66	78	66	43	26	28	87	64
10	95	01	54	10	65	32	71
94	87	94	43	41	65	43	26
33	87	65	34	28	38	46	33
41	23	41	76	54	38	91	43
27	54	83	27	65	88	37	64
17	11	19	76	48	18	45	17
84	54	31	76	35	84	32	58
36	76	23	54	68	20	36	14
24	53	24	56	78	94	23	12
12	67	54	21	89	43	47	12
56	87	56	43	24	76	51	43
77	86	34	25	61	77	43	27
19	87	65	19	23	47	57	32
28	28	51	67	34	28	48	42

Time ....

674	567	674	874	638	890	568
624	873	270	017	624	734	905
671	671	874	235	437	281	238
910	742	342	553	276	910	901
763	542	673	763	245	664	321
878	771	543	753	271	878	646
752	257	265	371	752	347	235
843	765	342	567	843	235	542
876	564	234	876	654	234	567
821	543	821	653	265	387	418
102	201	546	102	653	812	112
456	789	234	251	456	745	321
237	197	673	367	237	635	637
847	764	637	847	635	425	852
846	783	736	635	781	843	846
335	771	326	873	335	763	872
378	672	837	378	736	891	810
281	536	281	986	253	653	271
443	764	237	443	265	781	753
657	689	342	561	675	657	823

Time ....

516	615	516	893	625	847	782
827	827	651	825	837	653	445
745	873	754	745	755	432	891
653	763	563	566	653	365	871
874	198	235	471	874	236	714
654	564	445	645	654	384	251
843	256	345	761	918	843	348
118	881	818	453	116	118	342
822	522	782	282	882	822	768
845	352	764	238	845	458	326
874	187	874	784	237	453	267
187	234	118	553	178	187	456
465	345	564	456	465	234	265
876	456	345	234	237	876	678
781	871	765	187	465	781	118
123	132	123	546	781	432	234
567	543	234	567	765	576	891
562	562	265	256	786	198	234
776	667	676	891	776	453	234
765	664	678	765	654	367	918

Time ....

572	256	762	572	527	653	862
782	278	872	782	433	574	276
330	303	430	330	030	764	332
319	193	391	193	319	491	339
445	545	554	445	675	465	234
354	543	334	354	345	554	435
213	231	123	213	331	112	238
435	543	334	554	434	435	534
221	112	221	321	121	212	124
736	673	376	376	673	763	736
241	241	412	214	412	240	112
567	765	567	675	657	577	651
021	210	021	102	110	201	121
227	727	772	272	722	277	227
646	664	646	661	464	446	466
189	189	918	891	981	198	819
771	117	771	717	711	171	177
926	629	962	626	966	369	926
202	022	020	202	220	210	201
356	365	563	356	765	536	635

Time ....

119	991	191	116	910	199	119
553	335	353	553	331	551	354
012	120	102	021	012	104	211
482	484	482	248	428	824	842
216	612	621	261	216	126	616
527	725	275	527	752	257	572
2434	4426	6578	6754	2345	2434	2343
7876	7875	7867	7876	4567	3425	1987
3456	3456	7819	5432	7689	4563	2345
5682	3246	5621	5682	7621	8732	1956
1894	1948	1894	4526	7632	7682	1672
2214	2241	5622	6782	2211	2214	4124
5462	5462	8726	5672	7889	6532	0013
6781	1985	6721	6781	7628	9652	1934
5672	6582	8726	6738	6257	5267	5672
1872	1836	1872	8726	7627	1826	7827
2001	1002	0011	2001	1673	1020	1029
2679	8766	8687	6546	6437	2679	7443
7554	8664	5378	8676	7554	7676	5434
0864	0864	8765	7554	8775	5441	1644

Time ....

7543	8755	8541	7543	8754	6533	7632
8765	8764	8655	8765	6543	4654	5421
1654	5781	8653	7653	8753	8753	1654
8761	8764	7653	8762	7654	8761	8764
7663	8765	8875	7864	8764	5544	7663
8511	8765	1186	7641	8511	1894	6331
8631	8641	9864	8631	8613	8763	7631
8632	8763	8632	8764	8763	5438	5421
9841	8643	9841	0751	8643	8763	8763
8856	8654	8764	8856	8866	8685	6884
8674	8674	7863	6542	8734	8773	8764
1764	8641	1874	1763	1764	1457	8764
7237	7328	8753	6523	8642	7237	1876
2765	2864	6196	2765	7876	6543	7551
1287	1876	7765	5431	8641	1277	1287
5621	1976	7531	8734	5621	1256	8761
1987	8652	1987	1978	1874	6424	8763
7832	8783	8642	7823	8753	8742	7832
8753	8743	4865	8754	8753	6876	8723
1870	0986	1764	1708	1870	1077	1863

Time ....

8645	9875	1765	7875	8645	8723	8632
5765	5765	1776	8765	8764	8735	6878
8763	8754	8763	8723	8753	1874	1763
8765	7643	8756	7863	8765	8752	8763
1202	1022	1021	1202	1201	1276	8742
1853	7867	1864	1853	3257	6553	3547
5433	8763	5689	5433	3478	2346	8725
9742	9467	3685	8765	8765	4777	9742
7975	8754	8764	8764	7975	6346	6842
8763	8741	1874	8763	8641	7643	6781
7341	7341	8765	4567	2346	8765	3468
8652	8543	8652	4567	7654	8764	2356
8756	8754	8754	8756	7335	2564	8763
8764	8764	5421	7533	7643	8764	8768
6532	6135	5643	6532	6785	3477	8642
3455	3457	3486	3455	5543	2345	7532
5671	6531	2357	5436	1764	5671	6733
3477	4571	7642	3477	7763	6437	7538
2469	7432	1986	2469	9852	4579	7523
5743	9842	3670	4571	5743	6743	3567

Time ....

7523	6886	3567	4678	3478	5427	7523
8642	3568	8764	4588	8642	7543	3468
8531	6688	4488	8531	0165	1087	4671
8640	8650	6751	5571	7644	1753	8640
7301	1851	7410	7632	7301	0175	3466
3468	8532	4681	8751	3468	7631	8642
2457	7641	8643	4676	2457	8763	2475
7531	8641	3568	7643	1035	7531	8633
1875	1733	0567	8753	1875	8641	7432
8743	7532	7632	5688	8743	8753	3467
8755	8755	8875	5689	9755	4581	9751
8736	8761	8736	7754	7447	3568	7351
3468	7643	8875	3468	8753	1765	8441
1751	1750	1751	1741	8726	8763	8741
1977	1191	1977	7919	9771	8761	7791
8754	6754	8754	8547	8457	8744	8755
7653	7653	3367	3567	3567	5763	5368
1974	1974	1964	9147	7491	1947	1749
7864	7878	1755	7846	7864	4687	8746
8643	8648	8763	3486	8347	8643	3477

Time ....

8454	8455	8676	8454	4587	4584	8765
1175	1184	1765	1751	1157	1175	7641
8643	8637	8643	8641	4386	4368	8765
6432	2346	6433	6542	6432	3425	5432
8753	5784	8753	8762	4753	8735	3568
5241	8361	5412	7651	5241	8654	5242
7645	7654	7645	4765	5476	4577	5647
8411	8114	8411	1841	8711	4561	4811
8746	8764	4677	6488	7654	6874	8746
2574	2675	2574	2745	7452	4527	4452
7170	7701	7110	7171	7101	7170	0701
8741	7841	1874	8741	7814	1478	1784
4784	4788	4784	8747	8754	4784	4788
7632	7632	7623	2376	6737	2373	3728
3451	3434	3451	3541	1435	1543	5134
7633	7663	7336	7763	6733	7633	7636
8735	7853	6537	8735	8753	3578	9357

Time ....

CHAPTER NINE

META-GUIDING
TOWARDS 'PHOTOGRAPHIC MEMORY'
READING LEVELS

*The photographic imaging capacity of the human
eye is thousands of times more sophisticated than
the most advanced cameras. The full range of its
ability has yet to be explored.*

Open this book at any page, and glance at the page for one second – can you remember any word, graph, shape or sentence? Would you recognise the page again? As we know from the information on our amazing eyes, we *do* take the information in. We have to practise to remove the taught barrier that says we do not. Developing the skills mentioned in this chapter can assist you with this.

In Chapter 6, you were introduced to the basic elements of your using the visual guide. In this chapter, you will experiment with more advanced visually-guided movements that take into account your vertical as well as your horizontal peripheral vision.

These movements include 'reading backwards', reading in S's, reading in zig-zags, and reading down the centre sections of pages (as shown in Fig. 8).

These advanced techniques can be used for skimming and scanning, for previewing, for surveying, as exercises for increasing your reading speed, and as exercises for developing your peripheral vision. Persevere with your experimentation, and within one day to a week you will find significant improvements in all your reading.

It is especially useful to practise these techniques at very high speeds, for virtually no comprehension, before doing any reading. In this way you get your mind accustomed to high speeds. In such a preparation for reading, it is often useful to use the advanced guiding techniques on material that you have already read – in other words, accomplishing two tasks at once: reviewing what you have already read, while 'warming up' your brain for the task ahead. Before you take Self Test 4, it would be a good idea to skim through the entire text of what you have read so far of *Speed Reading* using your favourite advanced technique. To do this entire review give yourself a *maximum* of five minutes.

Following Self Test 4, our series of number exercises should help you develop awareness of both the vertical and horizontal nature of your vision. Each number group is consequently on two lines. Uncover the block of two numbers for a short glance. Write what you think you saw on the line.

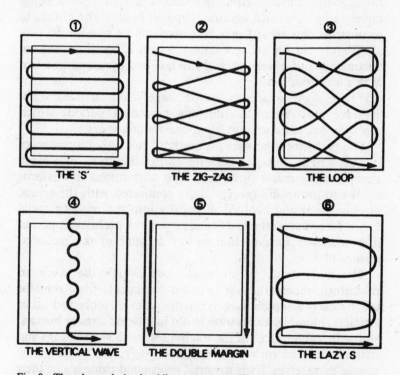

Fig. 8 The advanced visual guiding movements. The S, The Zig-zag, The Loop, the Vertical Wave, and the Lazy S can all be done at different speeds and with different depths of angle. For more in-depth reading, as much as 30 seconds per page can be taken. For training, surveying, previewing and reviewing, ten seconds a page should be a maximum. The double margin approach, in which either a finger or a thumb goes down the left margin, and your visual guide down the right hand margin, is useful primarily for reading, and can be varied by making either the left or right visual guide movement into a vertical wave

Check yourself. Practise this exercise either before or after the Self Test, or if you particularly like it, both!

The Prehistoric Period

1. Definition, Data, and Methods

History in its broadest sense should be a record of Man and his accomplishments from the time when he ceased being merely an animal and became a human being. The efforts to reconstruct this record may be classed under two heads:

(1) History (in the stricter sense), which is based on written documents and covers part of the last five thousand years of Man's activities, and

(2) Prehistory which is based largely on archaeological evidence and covers all the long preceding period, which probably amounts to more than one million years.

The prehistoric period is important, not only by reason of its vast length, but also because during this time Man made almost all his major discoveries and adaptations to environment and group-life (except those connected with the recent machine age) and evolved physically into the modern racial types. Hence at least a brief summary of the prehistoric period is a necessary introduction to any account of the recorded history of Man.

The main body of material upon which the work of prehistoric reconstruction is based comprises: first, remains left by early peoples, largely in the form of tools and other artifacts, found by excavation in old habitation sites or burials; secondly, other traces of their activities, such as buildings and rock-carvings or rock-paintings; and lastly, the bones of the people themselves. This material gives good evidence of their language. It can be supplemented to some extent – and with great caution – by a comparative study of the physical types, languages, and material culture of modern peoples.

The time when prehistory ends and true history begins varies in different parts of the world. Traditional history often covers the borderline between the two and can sometimes be successfully correlated with the archaeological evidence.

In prehistory, dates are entirely a matter of estimate and cannot be used as fundamental landmarks, as in the case of recorded history.

2. *The Origin of Man*

Man's place among the Animals. The various living and extinct species of Man are assigned by zoologists to the family Hominidae, which belongs to the sub-order Anthropoidea (containing monkeys, apes and baboons), of the order Primates (containing also Tarsius and the lemurs) of the class Mammalia. His nearest living relatives are the four genera of the family Simiidae (the so-called Anthropoid Apes): the gorilla and chimpanzee of equatorial Africa and the orang-utan and gibbon of south eastern Asia and the East Indies. Man is distinguished from the higher apes by the greater size of his brain (especially the forebrain), his fully erect position in walking, the better adaption of his hands for grasping and holding, and his use of language for communication.

Man's Animal Ancestors. No remains have yet been found of Man's immediate precursor, the primitive and more ape-like animal from which he is supposed to be descended. Neither have we yet found any certain traces of the postulated animal (often popularly termed the Missing Link) from which both Man and anthropoid apes are descended. Several forms of fossil apes have been found, however, which show a kinship to Man in some particulars and help to bridge over this gap: notably, Propliopithecus, from the Lower Oligocene of Egypt; Sivapithecus, from Miocene India; Dryopithecus, from Miocene France; and Australopithecus (the 'Taungs skull') from the Pliocene or Pleistocene of South Africa.

Date of Man's Origin. This has not yet been definitely established. The ancestors of the great apes and the ancestor of Man probably diverged from one another as early as the Miocene period, and Man acquired certain essentially human characteristics probably in the Pliocene period. The earliest known skeletal remains that are accepted as human are believed to date from the early or middle part of the Pleistocene period. For the purposes of the prehistorian, who has to rely largely on archaeological evidence, the record of Man may be said to begin at the moment when he was able to fashion the first stone tools which can be unmistakably recognised to be of human workmanship. This was early in the Pleistocene, or possibly in the very late Pliocene.

Place of Man's Origin. This is still entirely a matter of speculation. The old theory of Central Asia as the 'Cradle of Mankind' was based on false premises, which have been abandoned. From the distribution of the living and fossil great apes, it is thought that Man's divergence from the general anthropoid stem is likely to have taken place somewhere in the area comprising western Europe, the northern half of Africa, and southern Asia, with the preference perhaps slightly in favour of Africa or Asia, but there is not real evidence at present to warrant a final conclusion.

3. *Cultures and Their Dating*
a. *Cultures and Period*

Archaeological investigation of the material remains of prehistoric Man has shown that a wide variety of cultures flourished in different parts of the world and at different times. For convenience these have been grouped into a series of major cultures based primarily on the nature of the principal material used for implements (whether stone or one of the metals), and sometimes on the technique used in fashioning these implements. The oldest culture in the world was characterised by the use of chipped stone for implements and has been named Palaeolithic culture. Neolithic culture, on the other hand, was characterised by the use of polished stone implements; Bronze culture, by the use of bronze implements and so forth.

In most parts of the world the discovery and use of these different materials and techniques took place in a regular sequence in time. In the absence of fixed dates, it was thus found convenient to use these cultural terms in a chronological sense. Accordingly prehistoric times have usually been divided into the following series of periods of ages (beginning with the oldest):

Palaeolithic (old stone) characterised by chipped stone implements;

86

<u>Mesolithic</u> (Intermediate stone) a transitional period;
<u>Neolithic</u> (new stone) with polished stone implements;
<u>Chalcolithic</u> (Stone and copper) characterised by the first tentative use of copper implements;
<u>Bronze Age</u> with full development of copper and bronze implements; and
<u>Iron Age</u> with iron implements.

These names are excellent to identify cultures, but their use to designate periods of time has led to much inaccuracy and confusion, as the dates of the cultures to which they refer differ widely in different parts of the world. It is proper, for example, to speak of the Bronze Age of Hungary or some other limited area, where the beginning and end of the bronze culture can be fairly accurately dated. But it is quite impossible to speak with any meaning of the Bronze Age of the Old World for this period began some thousand or fifteen hundred years earlier in Mesopotamia, for instance, than it did in western Europe, and it gave way to the Iron Age one or two thousand years earlier in Asia Minor than in some parts of Siberia; while in Japan there was no true Bronze Age and in Australia no Bronze Age at all. The names of these periods are, however, too well established to be abandoned and are often useful, if employed with caution.

Stop Your Timer Now

Length of time .... mins

SELF TEST 4 (1,210 words)

1. History in its broadest sense should be a record of the evolution of life.　　　　True False

2. Pre-history is based largely on archaeological evidence.　　　　True False

3. Pre-history is important because Man made most of his discoveries and adaptation during this period.　　　　True False

4. Tools and artifacts found by excavation form a large part of our collection of the remains left by early peoples.　　　　True False

87

5. The division between pre-history and history is fairly constant geographically and chronologically.   True False

6. Living and extinct species of Man are assigned to the family Tarsius.   True False

7. Man's nearest living relatives are the four genera of the family Simiidae.   True False

8. Man's immediate predecessor remains a mystery.   True False

9. The date of Man's origin has been established within a period of a thousand years.   True False

10. The record of Man may be said to begin at the moment when he was able to fashion the first stone tool.   True False

11. The 'Cradle of Mankind' places Man's origin in central Asia.   True False

12. There is no real evidence to warrant a final conclusion on the place of Man's origin.   True False

13. Early cultures are identified by the growth of language and communication.   True False

14. The names of Ages such as Bronze and Iron have led to inaccuracy and confusion.   True False

15. The names of the periods of the development of Man should be abandoned.   True False

Comprehension .... Right

Percentage ....

N.B. – The remembering of material learnt while applying the study technique can be made much easier by using memory systems. I have covered this extensively in my book *Use Your Perfect Memory* (published by Dutton/Plume), donating a special section to examinations, and *Master Your Memory* (published by David & Charles).

27
91 ....

93
06 ....

92
11 ....

85
73 ....

05
92 ....

56
71 ....

29
65 ....

72
15 ....

02
47 ....

70
94 ....

38
67 ....

95
03 ....

52
17 ....

07
41 ....

84
20 ....

13
67 ....

34
55 ....

47
98 ....

17
09 ....

38
50 ....

73
32 ....

83
27 ....

99
31 ....

38
17 ....

46
12 ....

69
14 ....

93
74 ....

28
64 ....

60
29 ....

13
09 ....

84
26 ....

97
35 ....

82
41 ....

19
95 ....

10
86 ....

73
19 ....

47
04 ....

76
23 ....

19
75 ....

43
12 ....

06
84 ....

36
74 ....

14
96 ....

57
26 ....

32
81 ....

04
58 ....

74
90 ....

66
12 ....

64
27 ....

49
21 ....

92
61 ....

11
97 ....

62
59 ....

51
98 ....

19
58 ....

45
51 ....

40
39 ....

38
14 ....

82
39 ....

55
13 ....

93
015 ....

17
963 ....

67
921 ....

45
920 ....

03
961 ....

48
762 ....

90
216 ....

85
102 ....

92
183 ....

37
628 ....

77
69 ....

72
30 ....

13
76 ....

92
35 ....

17
935 ....

92
147 ....

24
095 ....

83
694 ....

97
276 ....

76
193 ....

03
184 ....

26
975 ....

59
413 ....

21
049 ....

75
941 ....

84
307 ....

18
592 ....

89
062 ....

56
107 ....

02
733 ....

75
916 ....

07
825 ....

81
943 ....

28
921 ....

42
105 ....

63
429 ....

90
472 ....

65
917 ....

82
457 ....

49
562 ....

94
165 ....

14
830 ....

93
724 ....

64
190 ....

93
076 ....

23
196 ....

36
741 ....

94
566 ....

56
029 ....

93
575 ....

38
470 ....

21
349 ....

93
059 ....

45
298 ....

36
275 ....

06
329 ....

12
965 ....

94
562 ....

51
379 ....

49
063 ....

10
692 ....

694
801 ....

937
804 ....

462
591 ....

905
817 ....

952
831 ....

31
280 ....

17
503 ....

94
705 ....

19
062 ....

29
410 ....

83
391 ....

77
152 ....

71
926 ....

62
831 ....

591
032 ....

152
407 ....

915
862 ....

105
762 ....

908
752 ....

328
947 ....

920
153 ....

845
701 ....

565
928 ....

724
016 ....

416
539 ....

286
910 ....

083
926 ....

167
528 ....

062
873 ....

941
570 ....

731
162 ....

492
184 ....

525
182 ....

462
731 ....

072
394 ....

862
143 ....

721
038 ....

157
924 ....

625
948 ....

483
109 ....

956
431 ....

762
457 ....

197
035 ....

482
191 ....

397
143 ....

920
413 ....

937
013 ....

710		062	
392	....	493	....
511		507	
936	....	341	....
829		173	
147	....	672	....
601		724	
934	....	162	....
290		407	
174	....	852	....
783		590	
420	....	743	....
593		421	
207	....	905	....
439		806	
617	....	944	....
127		704	
482	....	911	....
057		613	
982	....	936	....
162		730	
974	....	146	....
804		852	
193	....	901	....
253		394	
109	....	706	....

PART THREE

DEVELOPING ADVANCED
RANGE READING SKILLS

If you wished to devise a quick formula for developing advanced range reading skills, one of the simplest methods for so doing would be to do the opposite of everything you may have been taught and believed in relation to reading!

Consider the following beliefs:
1. Reading slowly and carefully leads to better comprehension.
2. Each word should be read as an individual unit.
3. Comprehension should be 100%.
4. Understanding should be 100%.
5. Memory of what has been read should be 100%.
6. Notes should be neat and written out along ruled lines in sentence form.
7. Finger-pointing is 'wrong' and slows you down.
8. Speeds of above 500 words per minute are impossible.
9. The faster reader comprehends, understands and appreciates less.
10. Higher speeds produce lower concentration.
11. Normal reading speeds are 'natural' and therefore the most appropriate.
12. Always read page 4 before you read page 5.
13. Immediately look up any vocabulary words you do not understand.
14. Problems or difficult areas in a book should be 'dealt with' before moving on.
15. Never subvocalise.
16. Sit still until you are finished.

All of the above are common misconceptions. The opposite of each is true!

In the following chapters, you will be given comprehensive guidelines on the *appropriate* use of your eye and brain for the advancement of complete Range Reading skills.

CHAPTER TEN

KEEPING THE BEAT – MULTIPLYING YOUR SPEED BY THE NEW METRONOME TRAINING METHOD

Your brain is a relativistic organ.

If you were driving along a motorway at 100 miles per hour, and your partner suddenly covered your speedometer and requested you to decellerate to 20 miles per hour, at what speed do you think you would 'level off', saying 'That's 20 miles per hour'?

Most people estimate between 40–60 mph and are correct.

The reason for this apparent absurdity is that the brain gets used to a *new norm*, and begins to compare all experiences with that norm. This relativistic nature of the brain can be applied to improving your reading speed. A metronome is the device you use, and it can be used in a number of ways. One is to allow each beat to indicate a single stroke along the line for your visual guide. In this way, a regular, steady, smooth reading rhythm can be established and maintained, and the usual decelleration in reading speed over time can be avoided. Once you have established a 'possible' reading speed, the metronome beat can be raised one beat per minute, and an improvement in your reading speed can be accomplished.

A second major use of the metronome is for relativistic Range Reading training. In this method of training, you set the metronome at abnormally high speeds, thereby obliging your eye/brain system to become accustomed to very high new norms. This form of training allows you to 'pull yourself up by the boot-straps' by establishing very high new norms, and by dipping below them into comfortably 'slow' reading speeds twice your previous average!

Following are our series of exercises designed to set you off on the high speed, high comprehension path!

Exercises

1. Exercise eye movements over page, moving eyes on horizontal and vertical planes diagonally upper left to lower right, and then upper right to lower left. Speed up gradually day by day. Purpose – to train eyes to function more accurately and independently.

2. Read normally for 5 minutes from a book which you will be able to continue using. Record wpm on the graph on page 14.

3. Practise turning 100 pages at approximately 2 seconds per page, moving eyes very rapidly down the page (2×2 min. sessions).

4. a Practise as fast as you can for 1 minute, not worrying about comprehension.
   b Read with motivated comprehension – 1 minute.
   c Calculate and record wpm on graph.
   Repeat as time allows.

5. Use any book (light material) of your choice, preferably one in which you are interested.
   Try for as much comprehension as possible, but realise that this exercise is concerned primarily with speed. In this exercise reading should continue from last point reached.
   a Practise-read for 1 minute at 100 wpm faster than your highest normal speed.
   b Practise-read 100 wpm faster than (a).
   c Practise-read 100 wpm faster than (b).
   d Practise-read 100 wpm faster than (c).
   e Practise-read 100 wpm faster than (d).
   f Practise-read with comprehension for 1 minute from point reached at end of (e). Calculate and record wpm on graph.

6. High Speed Practice 1
   a Use any easy book. Start from the beginning of a chapter.
   b Practise-read with visual aid, three lines at a time at a *minimum* of 2,000 wpm for 5 minutes.
   c Re-read to mark in 4 minutes.

d Re-read to mark in 3 minutes.

e Re-read to mark in 2 minutes.

f Read on from mark, for same comprehension as at (b) for 5 minutes.

g Read for normal comprehension for 1 minute. Record wpm on graph.

7. High Speed Practice 2

a Use any easy book, start at the beginning of a chapter.

b Scan for one minute, using visual aid, 4 seconds per page.

c Practise-read from the beginning at minimum of 2,000 wpm for 5 minutes.

d Repeat this exercise when possible.

e As 6g.

After you have completed a number of the Metronome Training exercises, go straight to Self Test 5 – The Major Musical Instruments.

Start Your Timer Now

SELF TEST 5

THE MAJOR MUSICAL INSTRUMENTS

The String Family

Nowadays, when we refer to the *strings*, we have in mind the violin family, consisting of four members – namely, the violin, the viola, the violoncello and the contra- or double-bass. These have many similar characteristics, but one of the chief differences is their size, ranging from the violin (the smallest), playing the highest notes, to the double-bass (the largest), playing the lowest notes. On all these instruments the strings are set in vibration with a bow, but sometimes the strings are plucked with the fingers. As the quantity of tone is not as great from stringed instruments as from wind instruments, many more string players than wind players are required in an orchestra. In a large symphony orchestra there might be as many as eighteen first violins, sixteen second violins, twelve violoncelli, and eight double-basses.

The shape of the violin, as we know it today, emerged during the middle of the 16th century, in Italy, having been gradually evolved from the rebec, a small bowed instrument of medieval times. The name *violin* was applied to all the members of this family, and not to the smallest one only. Louis XIV had a band of 'Twenty-four Violins' at his Court, and Charles II, on his return in 1660, set up a similar band in England. From this time the violin as such gained prestige in England, and the popularity of the viol gradually waned.

Plucked Instruments

It seems that the harp had its origin in prehistoric times, and might have come from the stretched string of an archer's bow, other strings of varying length (and pitch) being added, much in the same way as reeds or whistles were bound together to make a *syrinx* or pan pipes. The earliest evidence of a harp comes from Egypt and dates from the 13th century B.C.

The Harpsichord Family

The harpsichord was the most important of the keyboard instruments during the 16th, 17th and 18th centuries, holding a position analogous to that of the pianoforte of today. Three distinct instruments belong to the harpsichord family: the *virginal (or virginals)*, the *spinet*, and the *harpsichord* proper.

Fundamentally they are all harps placed horizontally, with their strings plucked by plectra operated from a keyboard.

Other major stringed instruments include the lute, the mandolin and the guitar. Those stringed instruments which are hit include the piano and the clavichord.

Wind Instruments

All wind instruments are made to sound by causing air to vibrate inside a hollow tube. Part of this tube must be open, so that the air inside the tube has contact with the surrounding air. The inside of the instrument, known as the bore, may be cylindrical (the same width throughout its length) or conical (small at one end and gradually increasing in width to the other), or it may be cylindrical for part of its length and conical for the remainder. The hollow tube may be straight or curved.

The choice of material for a wind instrument depends on a number of factors, such as its ability to stand the strain imposed on it during the various processes of its manufacture, its durability, its capacity for being bent or coiled, and its weight. The instrument when finished must be hard and rigid and the inside of the tube must be smooth.

Wind instruments were played in very ancient times. In fact, remains of bone flutes of the Later Stone Age have been found. We know from the Bible that the flute was played in Hebrew religious processions, with drums, tambourines and cymbals, and a ram's horn was blown on special occasions.

Over 3,000 years ago the Egyptians used trumpets on ceremonial occasions and later the Greeks, at the Pythian games, were holding contests for solo playing on the aulos, a double-reed instrument, related to the oboe. The Romans, too, had a kind of oboe, and tubas of different sizes.

Since early times wind instruments have been gradually modified and improved and the orchestral instruments of today are almost as perfect as they can be for our present needs; but there is no knowing what further changes might be made, if, for instance, composers were to demand instruments with quarter-tones.

Wood-Wind and Brass

Wind instruments are divided into two classes, the *wood-wind* and the *brass*. The term *wood-wind* does not signify that all the instruments in this class are made of wood; in fact, some are of ivory, of metal and of ebonite. Nor does the term *brass* mean that all these instruments are made of brass; there are some of silver, of copper, horn, ivory – and even wood!

The families of instruments generally regarded as wood-wind are: Flute, Oboe, Clarinet, Saxophone, Bassoon. The brass instruments are: Horns, Trumpets, Cornets, Trombones, Tubas. This classification is based on the method of production of the sound. No sound will be made by simply blowing through the tube: a generator must be used. There are three types of generators: the *free air-reed*, the *cane-reed* and the *lip-reed*.

If the sound is generated by *air-reeds*, as in the flute, or *cane-reeds*, as in the oboe or clarinet, the instrument is wood-wind.

If the sound is generated by the vibration of the lips against a cup-or-conical-shaped mouth-piece, the instrument is brass.

Percussion Instruments

Percussion instruments are members of an ancient instrumental family – perhaps the oldest. Some of its members still retain their primitive form in the modern orchestra. Instruments of percussion have always been popular in Asia and Africa, and instruments from these continents have found their way into Europe at three different periods in history. It seems that during the 12th, 13th, and 14th centuries the Crusaders were responsible for bringing the kettle-drums (then called nakers) to Europe. During the 18th century the popularity of 'Turkish music' in European armies introduced via Austro-Hungary, caused the addition of a variety of percussive instruments. From the First World War, with the influence of American-negro music on dance-music, further additions have been made. The percussion instruments include the drum family, the triangle, the cymbals and the gong, all of which have no definite pitch; and the tubular bells, the celesta, the glockenspiel, and the xylophone.

The Organ

The organ is said to have originated in Chaldea and Greece, where if first appeared as Pan Pipes or Syrinx. Reeds were cut off just below the knot, so that air blown down the reeds had to return to the open end. These were therefore stopped producing a note nearly an octave below that on an open pipe.

By making a slit in the knot, and a notch with a bevelled edge in the pipe just above the knot, a sound could be made by blowing through the lower end of the reed. Thus the whistle-form of open pipe came into being.

The reed pipe, although used in bagpipes in ancient times, was not used in the organ until the 15th century.

The whistle pipes were placed on a wooden box, the windchest, and the wind was supplied by two people who blew through flexible tubes. Unless the pipes were stopped by the player's hands or fingers, all the pipes sounded together.

The slider was next introduced. Each pipe was governed by a slider which was perforated, so that, on being drawn in or out, the wind to the pipe could be admitted or excluded. Next came a leather bag as a reservoir for the air, and later primitive forge bellows were used.

The Roman Hydraulus or water-organ came into being during the 3rd century B.C. By using the weight of water, the wind-supply system produced equal wind-pressure in the reservoir. Pipes were made of bronze and copper. There is evidence of a water organ which was in use during the 1st century B.C. It had one and a half octaves, with keys and three ranks of pipes, and produced 'Four-foot' pitch.

The organ was used for public feasts, and was not adopted for use in the Church until A.D. 450, when it was apparently used in Spain. In the 7th century it was used in Rome to improve the singing of the congregation. The art of organ-making was known in England in the 8th century. In the 10th century there was a large organ at Abingdon Abbey and another at Glastonbury. Winchester Cathedral had a famous organ of 400 pipes of brass and copper. There were two organists; probably one worked the levers to make the pipes sound, while the other worked the stop slides. Only one key at a time would have been used. The keys were three inches wide, and the organist was known as *pulsator-organum* ('organ-beater').

By the 14th century fixed organs came to be called *positif* or *positive*, in contrast to *portative* (portable) organs, which were, by this date, being used in processions in Germany and Italy. The keys were closer together by this time, and could be operated by the fingers of the player.

By the end of the 15th century the organ was developing into its modern form, with two manuals and a pedal-board. By the 16th century pipes of conical construction were in use, and the keys were small enough for an octave to be spanned by the player's hand.

During the 18th century, Jordan, an Englishman, enclosed a section of the organ in a box with a sliding front, thus allowing the tone to swell or diminish, hence the term 'swell-organ'. A marked development in the mechanism of the organ was made during the 19th century, whereby 'composition pedals', worked by the foot, enabled selected and fixed combinations of stops to be drawn. By developing the use of the pneumatic lever for operating heavy mechanism, the use of larger organs was made possible. More recently electric mechanisms have replaced the mechanical type, giving greater control with less effort, allowing the organist to concentrate on the musical effect.

Since 1930 the electronic organ has been in use; this has neither pipes nor wind, and it is claimed that by electrical production many tone-qualities can be produced at will. It occupies no more room than a grand piano, and is considerably cheaper than a pipe organ; its installation requires little more than its connection to an electric power plug. The popularity of the pipe organ, however, seems to have been little affected by the electronic organ.

Stop Your Timer Now

Length of time .... mins
SELF TEST 5 (1,760 words)

1. One of the chief differences in the string family is the relative size of the instruments. True False

2. There are more string players than wind players in an orchestra because the quantity of tone is not as great from stringed instruments. True False

3. The shape of the violin evolved from the viol. True False

4. When drawing-room music was the fashion a man of taste would often play the harp accompanied by his daughter or sister on the flute. True False

5. The earliest evidence of a harp comes from Egypt. True False

6. The virginal, spinet and harpsichord are all basically harps. True False

7. *All* wind instruments are made to sound by causing air to vibrate in a hollow tube.　True　False

8. In wind instruments the tube must be closed.　True　False

9. Wind instruments were developed after the Later Stone Age.　True　False

10. The instruments generally regarded as woodwind are clarinet, saxophone, bassoon, oboe, and flute.　True　False

11. Classification into wind and brass is based on the material used in producing the instrument.　True　False

12. An instrument is brass if its unit volume is louder than that of woodwind instruments.　True　False

13. The Crusaders were responsible for bringing kettle drums to Europe.　True　False

14. The Roman Hydraulus was a famous Roman musician.　True　False

15. The organ was adopted for use in the Church in A.D. 250.　True　False

Comprehension .... Right

Percentage ....

CHAPTER ELEVEN

MIND MAPPING – A NEW DIMENSION IN THINKING AND NOTE-TAKING

For centuries the human race has noted and recorded for the following purposes: memory; communication; problem solving and analysis; creative thinking; and summarisation, etc. The techniques that have been used to do this include sentences, lists, lines, words, analysis, logic, linearity, numbers, and monotonic (one colour) usage.

Good though some of these systems seemed, they have all used what you know to be the dominantly 'left cortical' thought modalities. When you begin to use these necessary elements in conjunction with rhythm, rhyme, form, dimension, colour, space and imagination, your skills in all mental areas will increase significantly and your mind will begin to reflect its true majesty.

How often have you seen 'the diligent student' hanging on every word that his teacher or professor utters, and faithfully recording each gem in his notebook?! It is a fairly common sight, and one that brings a number of negative consequences.

First the person who is intent on getting everything down is like the reader who does not preview – he inevitably fails to see the forest (the general flow of argument) for the trees.

Second, a continuing involvement with getting things down prevents objective and on-going critical analysis and appreciation of the subject matter. All too often note-taking by-passes the mind altogether.

And third, the volume of notes taken in this manner tends to become so enormous, especially when combined with added notes from books, that when it comes to 'revising', the student finds he has to do almost the complete task again.

Proper note-taking is not a slavish following of what has been said or what has been written, but is a selective process which should minimise the volume of words taken down, and maximise the amount remembered from those words.

To achieve this we make use of the 'Key-Word' concept. A Key-Word is a word that encapsulates a multitude of meanings in as small a unit as possible. When that word is triggered, the meanings spray free. It can be effectively represented by the diagram below.

Selecting Key-Words is not difficult. The first stage is to eliminate all the unnecessary surrounding language, so that if you came across the following statement in a science text: 'the speed of light has now been determined to be 186,000 miles per second' you would not write the whole sentence down but would summarise it as follows: 'light's speed = 186,000 m.p.s.'.

It is important to remember when making your notes with key-words that the Key-Words *must* trigger the right kind of remembering. In this respect words like 'beautiful', and 'horrifying', while being picturesque, are too general. They have many other meanings which might have nothing to do with the particular point you wish to remember.

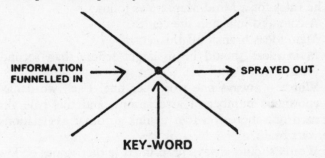

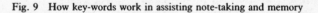

Fig. 9   How key-words work in assisting note-taking and memory

Further, a Key-Word should be one that you find personally satisfying and not one which you think somebody else might think is good. In many cases Key-Words need not be taken directly from the content of the lecture or the material being read. A word that you choose yourself and which summarises somebody else's words, is preferable.

If you practise Key-Word note-taking effectively you will be amazed at how much more information you can get into a given space.

The Mind Map – A New Dimension in Note-Taking

A Mind Map draws on all your mental skills: the Associative and Imagination skills from your memory; the words, numbers, lists, sequences, logic and analysis from your left cortex; the colour, imagery, dimension, rhythm, day-dreaming, Gestalt (whole picture) and spacial awareness abilities of the right side of your cortex; the power of your eye to perceive and assimilate; the power of your hand, with increasing skill, to duplicate what your eye has seen; and the power of your whole brain to organise, store, and recall that which it has learnt.

In Mind Map notes, instead of taking down what you wish to remember in the normal sentence or list-like fashion, you place an image in the centre of your note page (to help your concentration and memory) and then branch out in an organised fashion around that image, using Key-Words and Key Images. As you continue to build up the Mind Map, your brain creates an organised and integrated total map of the intellectual territory you are exploring.

The rules for a Mind Map are as follows:

1. A coloured image in the centre.
2. Main ideas branch off the centre.
3. Main ideas should be in larger letters than secondary ideas.
4. Words – always one word per line. Each word has an enormous number of associations, and this rule allows each one more freedom to link to other associations in your brain.
5. Words should always be printed (either upper or lower, or a combination of upper and lower cases).
6. Words should always be printed *on* the lines (this gives your brain a clearer image to remember).
7. Lines should be connected (this helps your memory to associate). The connected lines should be the same length as the word for efficiency of both association and space.
8. Use as many images as possible (this helps develop a whole-brained approach, as well as making it much easier for your memory; a picture *is*, in this context, worth a thousand words).
9. Use dimension wherever possible (things outstanding are

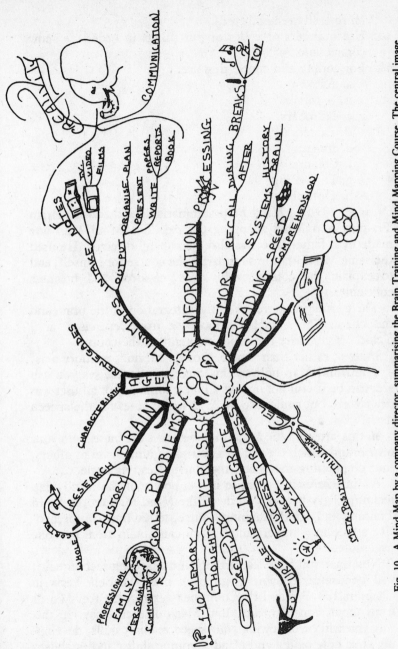

Fig. 10 A Mind Map by a company director, summarising the Brain Training and Mind Mapping Course. The central image refers to the integration of the brain and the body. The branches off the central image summarise the major elements of the course. Images, rather than words, provide succinct memory aids. This Mind Map was used both as a summary and review tool. It was also used as a means of presenting to other members of the company what had been gained during the course.

more easily remembered).

10. Use numbers or codes or put things in order, or show connections.
11. For coding and connecting use:
    a. Arrows
    b. Symbols
    c. Numbers
    d. Letters
    e. Images
    f. Colours
    g. Dimension
    h. Outlining

On page 109 is a Mind Map summarising a three-day Brain Training and Mind Mapping Course. The Mind Map was made by a father who was also a company director. He used the same Mind Map to summarise the course for himself, and to explain the course to his wife, children and business colleagues.

The central image refers to the integration of the brain and the body. The branches, clockwise from 'exercises' at 9 o'clock, summarise the major elements of the course.

Images, rather than words, provide succinct memory aids.

The Mind Map note of this three day course, as you can see, can be useful not only as a noted summary of all that was dealt with, but could also be used as the notes for the speech itself.

In this situation the Mind Map becomes the 'note from your own brain' which then allows you to communicate to others, thus completing the Speed and Range Reading cycle.

As an interesting exercise in the power of the Mind Map technique, try 'reading' in detail the Mind Map on the Brain Training and Mind Mapping Course, to see how comprehensive a summary/understanding you can obtain from this one page note.

Now that you have learnt the Mind Mapping technique, it will be useful for you to go back over the Self Tests in Chapters 1, 3, 7, 9 and 10. Continue to extract the Key-Words from them, and to make Mind Maps of each essay. In this way you will be reviewing your speed reading skills, developing your note taking and Mind Mapping skills, and establishing basic knowledge foundations in the fields of the brain, psychology, science, history and music.

As you continue through *Speed Reading*, make it a practice, after you have tested yourself on the Self Tests, to review them, underlining key words and concepts, and subsequently to Mind Map each article.

As a matter of interest finish this day's reading by thumbing through some of your old notes from school or other sources, observing how much was completely unnecessary, and how much time you could have saved first in writing them down, and second in reading them back. Many people find that only as little as 10% was necessary.

For a full explanation of the Mind Mapping Technique see *Use Both Sides of Your Brain* by the author.

CHAPTER TWELVE

USING KNOWLEDGE OF PARAGRAPH STRUCTURE TO INCREASE SPEED AND COMPREHENSION

By understanding the complexity of a part, you better understand the complexity of a whole. By understanding the complexity of a whole, you increase your ability to assimilate and understand everything.

In Chapter 8 we discussed the process of skimming in which certain pre-selected sections of the material are covered in order to gain a general overview. In this chapter we shall discuss the structure of the paragraph, thus enabling you to put into practice your skimming techniques appropriately.

Paragraphs, although looking very similar on the page as separated groups of words, are in fact tremendously varied within themselves. They range from the explanatory, through the descriptive, to the linking type. I am going to cover the most significant of these to give you a clear idea of how they can be approached, and shall give you general tips on methods you can use to help you get more out of the paragraphs you are reading.

Explanatory Paragraphs

Are those in which the writer has set out to explain a certain concept or point of view. They will generally be quite easy to recognise, and hopefully easy to understand. This type of paragraph tends to commence with a statement about what is to be explained, which is followed by a series of progressive steps to what we hope is a satisfactory conclusion. When coming across this type of paragraph you may rest reasonably assured that the first sentence or two will give you a general idea of what is going to be discussed, that the last sentence or two will contain the result or conclusion, and that the middle of the paragraph will contain details. Depending on your goal in reading, you will, in the initial skimming, be able to direct your attention appropriately.

Descriptive Paragraphs

Usually contain an expansion of ideas on a subject that has been introduced previously. Such paragraphs usually embellish, and as such are often not as important as those that introduce main elements. Of course there are exceptions in which the description of objects is vital, but in such cases you will usually be aware of this importance, and can focus your attention appropriately.

Linking Paragraphs

Are those which join others. As such they often contain key information, for they will summarise the contents of what has preceded and what follows. For example: 'The theory of evolution explained above will now be placed in the context of the latest developments in the field of biochemical genetic research.' In this brief sentence we have been given an extraordinary amount of information, information that gives us in capsule form the content of part of the material we are reading. Linking paragraphs, then, can be very useful as guides.

Structures of Paragraphs

There are of course numerous other types of paragraph, the three mentioned being among the most common. How can one make use of the structures of paragraphs and their placing in the text to improve one's reading efficiency?

Perhaps most important is to realise that in newspaper and magazine articles the first few paragraphs and the last few contain most of the significant information, the middle paragraphs containing particulars. If the material you are reading is of this type, concentrate, when skimming, on these paragraphs.

Other writers 'clear their throats' at the beginning before getting down to the meat of their presentation which is contained in the third or fourth paragraphs, and it is these of course on which the reader should concentrate initially.

There are also two 'games' that one can play with the

structure of paragraphs which help enormously in understanding and maintaining involvement.

The first of these is to make up, as you read, a memory word for the main theme and the secondary theme of each paragraph. This exercise forces you to remain involved with the material you are reading, making you think about the material as you read it. Your ultimate aim should be to develop the facility of selecting these words as you read without any pause or interruption to the flow of your reading.

It is possible, by using these key words, especially if placed in a Mind Map form to memorise the details of an *entire* book. Indeed, the key memory words, in conjunction with images, are the basic building blocks of your Mind Map. For more information on Mind Mapping, see *Use Both Sides of Your Brain*. For more information on advanced memory systems, see *Master Your Memory*.

The second of these paragraph 'games' is to relate, as you read through the paragraph, the first sentence to the remainder, asking yourself whether this is introductory, transitional or encompassing, or in some cases nothing to do with the words that follow it.

Before moving on to the previewing chapter read a number of different kinds of material to give yourself practice in the art of recognising different paragraph types.

CHAPTER THIRTEEN

PREVIEWING – YOUR MENTAL RECONNAISSANCE

Know the map if you wish to know the territory.

We come, in this chapter, to a concept at which we have been hinting all along: previewing material before it is read. The purpose of the preview is to develop a structure into which the mind can more easily fit the smaller details of that structure.

The previewer can be likened to a reconnaissance scout who goes ahead of the military force to determine the lay of the land, the position of the enemy forces, and areas of tactical advantage, etc. It is easier for an army to manoeuvre and operate in unknown territory if it has major reference points, and in the same way it is easier for the mind to attack or understand information once it has major landmarks to go by.

Previewing should be applied to whatever kind of material you are going to read, whether it be letters, reports, novels, or articles. It will in all cases speed up your overall reading and will improve your understanding because you will no longer be stumbling over items one after the other, but will be fitting pieces into a general picture.

Your approach to the preview should combine the elements that I mentioned in the chapters on skimming and paragraph structure. In other words, you will sensibly and rapidly go over the material you are about to read, selecting those areas most likely to hold the major chunks of information.

The concept of previewing as described here is for use in your general reading.

Your Self Test on Art – Primitive to Christian should mark a significant change in the way you read this kind of material. The previous chapters on Skimming, Scanning and Paragraph Structure combined with your awareness of the role of previewing, experience of the perception exercise and pushing up your speed, should enable you to tackle this reading task with a considerable degree of sophistication.

Before you get down to the main reading, *preview* this passage *very* rapidly, attempting to get the gist in a few seconds. When you are in the process of reading it, apply all the techniques you have learned, and as before push yourself to the limit of your ability, attempting to improve on your previous Self Test performances.

Start Your Timer Now

SELF TEST 6

ART – PRIMITIVE TO CHRISTIAN

Introduction

Art is one of the most profound expressions of the human brain. As such it is important that we all appreciate that from the beginning of history the mind behind the hand, behind the brush, was engaged in one of the most sophisticated and intricate forms of analysis and expression imaginable.

Primitive Art

It is essential for the observer to have at least an outline background of the historical development of pictorial art, and to take first a brief glance at its prehistoric and primitive forms. All the arts have their origin in prehistoric times, but the representations of animals incised on ivory and bone or drawn and painted on the walls and ceilings of caves in the north of Spain and south of France still excite wonder by their exceptional power and 'modernity'. Masterpieces were produced between (to give very rough limits) 40,000 B.C. and 10,000 B.C. What we notice in the photographs or outline copies made from them is the way in which the artists have selected and emphasised the main characteristics of the animals – mammoth and bison, deer, wild boar and wild horse – depicted; the knowledge they display of their anatomy; the solid bulk and vigorous movements they convey with no more than a little black and red ochre.

The period during which they were produced is longer than all recorded history, but there are comparable paintings and drawings by people living a similar life at a much later date. Thus the African bushman has left, in rock-shelters, drawings of animals as beautiful as those of our first European artists and resembling them in style, though some are as recent as the 19th century of our era. The realism of these hunting folk is not repeated in the art of the next stage of civilisation, when social life takes a more definite form, when tools of stone and bronze are perfected, the crafts of pottery and weaving are pursued and, with the growth of agriculture, various rites and ceremonies propitiating the elements come into being. The typical primitive society, of which there still remain various survivals as in Polynesia, is largely concerned in the arts with its rudimentary religion. Carving and sculpture exceed painting in importance: the idol in three dimensions is thought more impressively to represent the powers assumed to affect primitive life. Painting and drawing became a series of signs and symbols.

The Ancient Mediterranean World

Painting and drawing in the ancient Mediterranean world has three aspects. There is first the wall painting, with bold outline and flat colour, the technique somewhat resembling that of certain modern posters. The ancient Egyptians used it on the exteriors of their temples: a sharply defined low relief providing an outline which was filled with bright colour. The majority of surviving Egyptian paintings are those of tomb walls, including scenes from the life of the deceased. A number of conventional devices are regularly used, for example, the male figure is painted in red ochre, the female, in yellow; the head and legs are always in profile however otherwise the body is turned. A great quality, however, is the lively observation which appears in scenes of banqueting and dancing or fishing and fowling along the Nile. The wall paintings of ancient Crete discovered in the palace of Knossos afford a parallel with those of Egypt in their bright, flat colours and decided outlines, though entirely secular in character.

The painted pottery of ancient Greece offers on a small scale something of these traditional styles. The male figure is dark, the female figure light, and outline plays a dominant part. The Greek vase painters (who often signed their cups and vases) can be studied as draughtsmen with a most exquisite sense of value of line and silhouette. In the classical period, however, the art of vase painting ceased to occupy an important place, and it is now that we first come upon the record of pictures in the modern sense, though our idea of them is unfortunately not based on the authentic works of the legendary masters, Zeuxis or Apelles, but on copies of Greek painting discovered when the Roman cities Pompeii and Herculaneum were excavated. It is clear enough, however, that the Greek painters had given the art a scope and character undreamed of by the Egyptians or Minoans. Their work was no longer flat, but represented light and shade. The Greeks conceived dramatic figure compositions; they interested themselves in the problem of giving individual character and expression to their figures, in features and gesture. The Greco-Roman works that adorned the villas of wealthy Romans in the 1st century A.D. provide examples of landscape (previously unknown) and of still-life studied for its own sake. They forecast the later development of painting in Italy.

Byzantine Art

The dissolution of the Roman Empire, the establishment of a new Rome in the former Byzantium (Constantinople), and the emergence of Christianity as the universal creed of the West gave to painting a new character, spirit and aim. The Christian religion was now the artist's theme. A formal style now known as Byzantine, suited to express its earnestness and ritual, grew up. Constantinople had many links with the East, whose influence is to be seen in the use of rich colour.

The main triumphs of Byzantine pictorial art were achieved in mosaic, on the walls or the curved surface of the inner domes of the Byzantine church. Its other forms were, firstly, the icon, the image of Christ or the Virgin, represented, of set purpose, in a fixed convention which in itself declared the unalterable nature of belief; and secondly the illumination of manuscript Gospels and liturgical works with painting and gold. The style of these is as unchanging as that of the icon.

The Byzantine capital remained intact, prosperous and fixed in its ways for 1,100 years after its foundation in the 4th century A.D., so that works very similar in many respects may vary considerably in date. The sphere of Byzantine art corresponds to the sphere of influence of the Byzantine Empire: the eastern shores of the Mediterranean, Greece and the Greek islands. To some extent it was carried westward, with the movements of Byzantine missionaries and craftsmen. The famous 8th-century Irish manuscript, the Book of Kells, has its links of style with the eastern Mediterranean. The Italian cities Florence, Siena and Pisa had a Byzantine tradition, the end of which is marked by the painting of Cimabue in Florence and Duccio in Siena in the 13th century. In eastern Europe what is now Yugoslavia has remarkable Byzantine wall paintings of the 12th to 14th centuries. Greek painters introduced the icon into Russia and the Russian Andrew Roublev (c. 1360–c. 1430) brought the style to a magnificent pitch of development. Crete remained a centre until the 16th century and there is still a trace of the Byzantine tradition in the paintings of El Greco (c. 1545–1614).

Early Christian Art in the West

East or West, early Christian art in general avoided the realistic imitation of the human form that had been a feature of classical art. Yet it was not necessarily crude and imperfect, but more spiritual and abstract, in the sense of being removed from mundane affairs; and from this point of view it is nowadays judged more favourably than it used to be. Early Christian art in the West has an intricate history. It followed first the Greco-Roman tradition as in the paintings of the Roman catacombs. It was modified by the local character of the various regions into which the Roman Empire was regrouped. It was affected by its communications, religious and commercial, with the Eastern Empire. The monastic art of the illuminated manuscripts was for a long time the main form of pictorial art, as in Celtic and Anglo-Saxon Britain and in the empire of Charlemagne. Two things became increasingly clear with time: that Christianity was the one unifying and educational force in Europe, and that pictures were a principal means of conveying its message effectively and universally among people speaking different tongues or unable to read and write. With the great period of church building, from the 11th century, the international western style known as Romanesque developed. Its greatest products were the wall paintings of churches. Working on a large area, the painters developed a bold and simple style of much grandeur.

Stop Your Timer Now

Length of time .... mins

SELF TEST 6 (1,415 words)

1. All the arts have their origin in prehistoric times.   True False

2. 'Masterpieces' were produced even by primitive men.   True False

3. The African bushman, unlike the caveman, did not concern himself so much with animals.   True False

4. The typical primitive society is largely concerned in the arts with religion.   True False

5. Early religion made art more symbolic.   True False

6. Ancient Mediterranean wall painting is distinguished by fine outlines and brilliant colours.   True False

7. Egyptian paintings made use of a number of conventional devices.   True False

8. In the classical period of Greek painting the vase occupied an important place.   True False

9. Much of our knowledge of this period is based on the work of the Greek masters Zeuxis and Apelles.   True False

10. The Greeks were not particularly concerned with the representation of light and shade.   True   False

11. Byzantine art made Christianity the artists' theme.   True   False

12. The links of Constantinople with the East can be seen in Byzantine art in the rich colour.   True   False

13. The Byzantine school lasted approximately 500 years.   True   False

14. Early Christian art in the West attempted to imitate the human form realistically.   True   False

15. The Romanesque style developed in conjunction with an increase in church building.   True   False

Comprehension .... Right

Percentage ....

CHAPTER FOURTEEN

DEVELOPING YOUR MASTERMIND VOCABULARY (I)

Prefixes and Exercises

The improvement of vocabulary is, historically, one of the most important factors in the raising of the level of human intelligences.

Having dealt with our introductory material, the theory behind eye movements and the major problem areas in reading, we now move on to the first of three sections on vocabulary. This factor is generally considered to be the most important individual item in the development of efficient reading. It is perhaps not so surprising when one realises that the extent of one's vocabulary is an indication of the extent of one's knowledge, which in turn is an indication of the amount of material that one has been able to assimilate and read.

Schools, colleges and universities include general vocabulary testing as one of the major criteria by which they judge the suitability of applicants, and the success or failure of a student often depends on his ability to understand and use words properly.

The importance of vocabulary extends, of course, far beyond the academic world: the businessman who has at his command a wider range of words that his peers is at an immediate advantage, and the person who, in social situations, can both understand easily and comment creatively also has the upper hand.

Before getting down to the practical side I should like to mention another important point. Most of us have more than one vocabulary. In fact we usually have at least three. First is the vocabulary we use in *conversation*, and in many cases this may not exceed 1,000 words (it is estimated that in the English language there are well over 1,000,000 words).

Our second vocabulary is the one we use when *writing*. This tends to be larger than the spoken one, because more time is devoted to the construction and content of sentences, and because there is less pressure on the writer.

The largest of our three vocabularies is our *recognition* vocabulary – the words that we understand and appreciate when we hear them in conversation or when we read them, but which we ourselves may not use either in writing or in conversation. Ideally, of course, both our speaking and our writing vocabularies should be as large as our recognition vocabulary, but in practice this is seldom the case. It is possible, however, to increase all three quite drastically.

The purpose of this chapter is to introduce to you over eighty prefixes (letters, syllables, or words placed at the commencement of a word). As our English language has a large element of Greek and Latin, you will note that many of the prefixes are taken from these two languages.

Study the following list thoroughly. A complete understanding of it will give you the key to thousands of unfamiliar words. In later chapters you will find a similar coverage of suffixes and roots. For a method of memorising perfectly this list and the lists in Chapters 15 and 16 refer to *Master Your Memory* by the author.

Vocabulary Mastermind Exercises

Following the prefixes are three vocabulary exercises designed to give you practice with your new knowledge. These exercises are not vocabulary tests in the strict sense. In many cases definitions have been 'stretched' a little in order to include a key word that carries an appropriate prefix.

When doing this exercise break up each of the words which you select, trying to establish its meaning from its structure. To help you with this, have a dictionary at hand.

When you have filled in each of the fifteen blank spaces with the letter of the word you think is correct, check your answers on pages 183 and 184.

PREFIXES

G=Greek, L=Latin, F=French, E=English

Prefix	Meaning	Example
a-, an- (G)	without, not	anærobic
ab-, abs- (L)	away, from, apart	absent
ad-, ac-, af- (L)	to, towards	advent, advance
aero-	air	aeroplane, aeronaut
amb-, ambi- (G)	both, around	ambiguous
amphi- (G)	both, around	amphitheatre
ante- (L)	before	antenatal
anti- (G)	against	antidote, antitoxic
apo- (G)	away from	apostasy
arch- (G)	chief, most important	archbishop, archcriminal
auto- (G)	self	automatic, autocrat
be-	about, make	belittle, beguile, beset
bene- (L)	well, good	benediction
bi- (G)	two	biennial, bicycle
by-, bye- (G)	added to	by ways, bye-laws
cata- (G)	down	catalogue, cataract
centi-, cente- (L)	hundred	centigrade, centenary
circum- (L)	around	circumference, circumambient
co-, col-, com-, cor-	together	companion
con-, (L)	with,	collect, co-operate
contra- (L)	against, counter	contradict, contraceptive
de- (F)	down	denude, decentralise
deca-, deci- (G)	ten	decade, decagon
demi- (L)	half	demigod
dia- (G)	through, between	diameter
dis- (L)	not, opposite to	dislike, disagree
duo- (G)	two	duologue, duplex
dys- (G)	ill, hard	dysentry
e-, ex-	out of	exhale, excavate
ec- (L)	out of	eccentric
en-, in-, em-, im-, (L; G) (F)	into, not	enrage, inability, embolden, emulate, impress
equi-	equally	equidistant
epi- (G)	upon, at, in addition	epidemic, epidermis
extra- (L)	outside, beyond	extra-essential
for-, fore- (E)	before	foresee
hemi- (G)	half	hemisphere
hepta- (G)	seven	heptagon
hexa- (G)	six	hexagon, hexateuch
homo- (L)	same	homonym
hyper- (G)	above, excessive	hypercritical, hypertrophy
il-	not	illegal, illogical
in-, im-, (un) (L, G, F)	not	imperfect, inaccessible
inter- (L)	among, between	interrupt, intermarriage
intra-, intro- (L)	inside, within	intramural, introvert
iso- (G)	equal, same	isobaric, isosceles
mal- (L)	bad, wrong	malfunction, malformed
meta- (G)	after, beyond	metabolism, metaphysical
mis-	wrongly	misfit, mislead

mono- (G)	one, single	monotonous, monocular
multi- (L)	many	multipurpose, multimillion
non-	not	nonsense, nonpareil
ob-, oc-, of-, op- (L)	in the way of resistance	obstruct, obstacle, oppose
octa-, octo (G)	eight	octahedron, octave
off-	away, apart	offset
out-	beyond	outnumber, outstanding
over-	above	overhear, overcharge
para- (G)	aside, beyond	parable, paradox
penta- (G)	five	pentagon, pentateuch
per- (L)	through	perennial, peradventure
peri- (G)	around, about	perimeter, pericardium
poly- (G)	many	polygamy, polytechnic
post- (L)	after	postscript, postnatal
pre- (L)	before	prehistoric, pre-war
prime-, primo- (L)	first, important	primary, Prime-Minister
pro- (L)	in front of, favouring	pronoun, protect
quadri-	four	quadrennial, quadrangle
re- (L)	again, back	reappear, recivilise
retro- (L)	backward	retrograde, retrospect
se-	aside	secede
self-	personalising	self-control, self-taught
semi- (G)	half	semicircle, semidetached
sub- (L)	under	submarine, subterranean
super- (L)	above, over	superfluous, superior
syl-	with, together	syllogism
syn-, sym (G)	together	sympathy, synchronise
tele- (G)	far, at or to a distance	telegram, telepathy
ter- (L)	three times	tercentenary
tetra- (G)	four	tetrahedron, tetralogy
trans- (L)	across, through	transatlantic, translate
tri- (L; G)	three	triangle, tripartite
ultra- (L)	beyond	ultramarine, ultra-violet
un- (im) (L, G, F)	not	unbroken, unbutton, unable
under-	below	underfed, underling
uni- (L)	one	unicellular, uniform
vice- (L)	in place of	viceroy, Vice-President
yester- (E)	preceding time	yesterday, yesteryear

Vocabulary 1 (a)

1. .... is reserved for the most important and most dangerous of one's opponents.
2. A .... is a two footed animal.
3. A person or thing beyond comparison, a model of excellence, is known as a ....
4. Streams that flow together are said to be ....
5. A coalition of three men for purposes of government or administration is called a ....
6. Many people in the world are not able to read; they are ....

7. .... is the introduction of one substance into another.
8. Because people estimated that this creature had 100 legs, they called it a ....
9. .... means third in rank, order, or succession.
10. One opposite of fascination is ....
11. To go against restrictions laid down is to .... the rules.
12. A creature that can live in both air and water is called an ....
13. .... means operating in a backward direction.
14. A .... is a person who speaks many languages.
15. If you have a strong feeling against something you are said to be ....

a. polyglot   b. amphibian   c. disenchantment   d. centipede
e. biped   f. confluent   g. illiterate   h. antipathetic
i. retroactive   j. contravene   k. tertiary   l. archenemy
m. paragon   n. triumvirate   o. impregnation

Vocabulary 1 (b)

1. One who does not believe in God is an ....
2. He was a .... because he had a fixation on a single subject.
3. The Ten Commandments are often called the ....
4. An outstanding object or person is said to be ....
5. A plane figure with eight sides and angles is known as an ....
6. To .... means to dig away the foundations, to bring down from below.
7. A .... is a graveyard below ground.
8. A person who .... gives up a claim, resigns, gets away from a situation,
9. An injection into the returning blood stream is called an .... injection.
10. When something gets in the way of light or meaning, it is said to ....
11. To consider one's self to be above others is to possess a .... attitude.
12. The medical condition in which one loses one half of one's field of vision is known as ....

13. A .... is an instrument that enables observers to look over an object.
14. A line on a map which connects those places having equal average temperature is called an ....
15. An .... is a person who writes his own life story.

a. intravenous b. autobiographer c. abdicates
d. Decalogue e. atheist f. undermine g. supercilious
h. isotherm i. monomaniac j. octagon k. catacomb
l. obfuscate m. periscope n. prominent o. hemianopsia

Vocabulary 1 (c)

1. A dividing membrane between two areas is called a ....
2. .... applies to what is immaterial, incorporeal, supersensible, beyond the physical.
3. A .... is a curse.
4. To .... means to bring up or throw back from a deep place; to vomit.
5. A .... is someone who is of no importance.
6. An ancestor may also be called a ....
7. When something passes through, permeates, extends and is diffused, it is said to ....
8. If you ...., you are going beyond ordinary limits.
9. A verse containing five feet is called a ....
10. .... is charity, kindness or generosity.
11. If you are prudent and wary, and look all around before doing anything you are ....
12. Something capable of being calculated beforehand is ....
13. That which has existed from the beginning, we call ....
14. To .... means to subdue by superior force; to bring under the yoke.
15. If we interpret something wrongly, we .... it.

a. metaphysical b. regurgitate c. forebear d. extravagate
e. misconstrue f. primordial g. circumspect h. diaphragm
i. subjugate j. predeterminable k. nonentity l. pentameter
m. beneficence n. pervade o. malediction

CHAPTER FIFTEEN

DEVELOPING YOUR MASTERMIND VOCABULARY (II)

Suffixes and Exercises

The use of increasingly complex and sophisticated language structures, and the units (vocabulary) that go to make up those structures, is one of the defining characteristics of evolutionary development. The nurturing and training of your skill in this area is your natural right, your own responsibility, and a rare opportunity which, if grasped, will provide you with exceptional benefits. Claim it. Accept it. Do it.

In Chapter 14 we discussed vocabulary in general, mentioning the tremendous importance it plays in reading efficiency, and the emphasis that is placed on it by educational institutions.

The fact that we have three different vocabularies, recognition, writing and speaking, was also covered and it was stressed that each of these three should be improved. At the end of the chapter I introduced you to eighty-seven prefixes which were then tested.

By now your facility with this building block of vocabulary, especially if you have used the information you have so far gathered from *Speed Reading* will have increased considerably and you will be ready for the nest step in vocabulary building. This is to learn the suffixes (letters, syllables, or words placed at the end of a word). As in the section on prefixes you will notice that most suffixes are taken from the Latin and the Greek.

Vocabulary Mastermind Exercises
Following the list of fifty-one suffixes you will find a number of vocabulary tests similar to those you did in Chapter 14. After having learnt the suffixes and completed the vocabulary

tests to your satisfaction, browse through a good dictionary, studying the various ways in which these suffixes are used. Keep a record of exceptionally good examples or examples which you find interesting and useful.

SUFFIXES

G=Greek, L=Latin, F=French, E=English

Suffix	Meaning	Example
-able, -ible (L)	capable of, fit for	durable, comprehensible
-acy (L; G)	state or quality of	accuracy
-age (L)	action or state of	breakage
-al, -ial (L)	relating to	abdominal
-an (ane, ian) (L)	the nature of	Grecian, African
-ance, ence	quality or actions of	insurance, corpulence
-ant (L)	forming adjectives of quality, nouns signifying a personal agent or something producing an effect	defiant, servant
-stable (L)	See -able, -ible	
-arium, -orium (L)	place for	aquarium, auditorium
-ary (L)	place for, dealing with	seminary, dictionary
-ate (L)	cause to be, office of	animate, magistrate
-ation, -ition (L)	action or state of	condition, dilapidation
-cle, -icle (L)	diminutive	icicle
-dom (E)	condition or control	kingdom
-en (E)	small	mitten
-en (E)	quality	golden, broken
-er (E)	belonging to	farmer, New Yorker
-ess (E)	feminine suffix	hostess, waitress
-et, -ette (L)	small	puppet, marionette
-ferous (L)	producing	coniferous
-ful (E)	full of	colourful, beautiful
-fy, -ify (L)	make	satisfy, fortify
-hood (E)	state or condition of	boyhood, childhood
-ia (L)	names of classes, names of places	bacteria, America
-ian (L)	practitioners or inhabitants	musician, Parisian
-ion (L)	condition or action of	persuasion
-ic (G)	relating to	historic
-id(e) (L)	a quality	acid
-ine (G; L)	a compound	chlorine
-ish (E)	a similarity or relationship	childish, greenish
-ism (G)	quality or doctrine of	realism, socialism
-itis (L)	inflammation of (medical)	bronchitis
-ist (G)	one who practises	chemist, pessimist
-ity, -ety, ty (L)	state or quality of	loyalty
-ive (L)	nature of	creative, receptive
-ize, -ise (G)	make, practise, act like	modernise, advertise

-less (E)	lacking	fearless, faceless
-logy (G)	indicating a branch of knowledge	biology, psychology
-lent (L)	fulness	violent
-ly (E)	having the quality of	softly, quickly
-ment (L)	act or condition of	resentment
-metry, -meter (G)	measurement	gasometer, geometry
-mony	resulting condition	testimony
-oid (G)	resembling	ovoid
-or (L)	a state or action, a person who, or thing which	error, governor, victor, generator
-ous, -ose (L)	full of	murderous, anxious, officious, morose
-osis	process or condition of	metamorphosis
-some	like	gladsome
-tude	quality or degree of	altitude, gratitude
-ward (E)	direction	backward, outward
-y (E)	condition	difficulty

Vocabulary 2 (a)

1. .... is the condition of being marked with disgrace.
2. A .... is a woman who governs a nunnery.
3. Someone who has very strong nationalistic feelings and who makes a practice of this somewhat exaggerated patriotism is called a ....
4. That which is intractable, unruly, perverse; which goes in the wrong or unpredictable direction is ....
5. A .... is one who works in a certain field, such as medicine.
6. A .... is a comment or statement which has a high degree of insipidity and triteness.
7. The unpleasant medical condition in which part of the testicle becomes irritated and inflamed is known as ....
8. To .... is to imbue with the added qualities of courage, inspiration and fearlessness.
9. The doctrine of pursuing pleasure as the highest good is known as ....
10. If you are capable of working twelve hours a day without a rest; if you can engage in physical exercise for hours without seeming to get tired, then you are ....
11. Handwriting which is in the nature of a running hand; which forms the character rapidly without raising the pen

is known as .... handwriting.
12. A .... is a small ornamental design, drawing or picture.
13. The quality or state of being uppermost, of having complete authority or power, is the state of ....
14. To .... is to render something unable to operate or move; to disband.
15. .... is the state of being bound or tied to something, either physically or mentally.

a. indefatigable   b. vignette   c. demobilise   d. epididymitis
e. practitioner   f. ignominy   g. supremacy   h. platitude
i. untoward   j. cursive   k. Chauvinist   l. prioress
m. hedonism   n. embolden   o. bondage

Vocabulary 2 (b)

1. Someone who places himself in a condition of suffering for his beliefs, is placing himself in a position of ....
2. A diminutive particle of matter is sometimes known as a ...., although this term now usually applies to the small particles constituting blood.
3. A girl who is joyful, attractive and engaging is ....
4. A charge for something which relates to the lowest or smallest price is ....
5. .... is the process in which fluids tend to mix, even though porous membranes.
6. A .... is a place where one goes to see models or projections of the solar system and other sections of the universe.
7. People who speak loudly and often are ....
8. .... is the state of being exhausted.
9. A rude girl or tomboy is said to be ....
10. A .... person is full of antagonism and the desire to quarrel or fight.
11. A place where birds are kept is known as an ....
12. A .... look is one full of mischief or malice.
13. A .... is a person who holds high rank or status.
14. To be gentle, quiet, peaceful and serene is to be ....

15. An .... is that which provokes or produces discomfort or inflammation.

a. winsome b. minimal c. irritant d. enervation
e. vociferous f. bellicose g. aviary h. corpuscle
i. magnate j. hoydenish k. baleful l. placid
m. osmosis n. planetarium o. martyrdom

Vocabulary 2 (c)

1. To be filled with the desire to do nothing, to be lazy, phlegmatic and idle is to be ....
2. A .... is an eloquent speaker or writer.
3. The .... is that class of educated people who tend to form much of public opinion.
4. .... relates or pertains to the constant chemical changes in living matter.
5. An .... is any creature which resembles Man.
6. The branch of knowledge which deals with the body's organs and their functions is ....
7. A synonym for a state of boldness, courage and robustness is ....
8. That which is 'of the nature of the world' is often said to be ....
9. A disease the qualities of which are plague-like and virulent is often called a ....
10. .... is the act of having a contract or marriage abolished.
11. To look at one's self .... is to have the quality of the vain god who fell in love with his reflected image.
12. To .... is to raise to a higher or more extreme degree.
13. When we attribute to someone or something the quality of god-head we make him or it a ....
14. Someone whose appetites can not be satisfied is ....
15. The branch of knowledge which deals with the human mind and its functioning is ....

a. mundane b. narcissistically c. intelligentsia
d. insatiable e. intensify f. rhetorician g. deity
h. psychology i. physiology j. pestilence k. hardihood
l. annulment m. anthropoid n. metabolic o. indolent

CHAPTER SIXTEEN

DEVELOPING YOUR MASTERMIND VOCABULARY (III)

Roots and Exercises

The pen is mightier than the sword only if the brain behind it knows how to wield the word.

This is the last of the vocabulary chapters and it deals with word roots (words from which others are derived).

As in the earlier chapters dealing with vocabulary, a list is given, this time of word roots, their translated meanings, and an example of a word containing the root. This is followed by the kind of vocabulary test with which you have now become familiar.

Five Steps for Continuing Mastermind Vocabulary Improvement

As this is the last chapter dealing with words and their meanings, I should like to offer a few hints on how you may continue to improve your vocabulary:

First, perform the exercise mentioned in Chapter 15; that is, browse through a good dictionary, studying the various ways in which the prefixes, suffixes and roots you have learnt are used. Keep a record of noteworthy examples and useful words. (If you own one, keep this record in the creative development section of the Universal Personal Organiser (UPO) Tony Buzan diary system.)

Second, make a continuing and concentrated effort to introduce into your vocabulary at least one new word a day. New words are retained only if they are repeated a number of times, so once you have selected your word or words make sure that you use them often and effectively.

Third, be on the look-out for new and exciting words in conversations. If you are embarrassed about asking a speaker to define his terminology, make a quick mental note or jot the word down and look it up later.

Fourth, keep an eagle-eye out for unfamiliar words in anything you read. *Don't* write them down as you read, but make a mark with a pencil as indicated in Chapter 4 and look them up afterwards.

And **finally** if you feel so inclined, go to your local bookshop or library and ask for a book on vocabulary training – there are a number and most of them are quite helpful.

ROOTS

LATIN AND GREEK

Root	Meaning	Example
aer	air	aerate, aeroplane
am (fr. amare)	love	amorous, amateur, amiable
ann (fr. annus)	year	annual, anniversary
aud (fr. audire)	hear	auditorium, audit
bio	life	biography
cap (fr. capire)	take	captive
cap (fr. caput)	head	capital, per capita, decapitate
chron	time	chronology, chronic
cor	heart	cordial
corp	body	corporation
de	god	deify, deity
dic, dict	say, speak	dictate
duc (fr. ducere)	lead	aqueduct, duke, ductile
ego	I	egotism
equi	equal	equidistant
fac, fic (fr. facere)	make, do	manufacture, efficient
frat	brother	fraternity
geo	earth	geology
graph	write	calligraphy, graphology, telegraph
loc (fr. locus)	place	location, local
loqu, loc (fr. loqui)	speak	eloquence, circumlocution
luc (fr. lux)	light	elucidate
man (fr. manus)	hand	manuscript, manipulate
mit, miss (fr. mittere)	send	admit, permission
mort (fr. mors)	death	immortal
omni	all	omnipotent, omnibus
pat (fr. pater)	father	paternal
path	suffering, feeling	sympathy, pathology
ped (fr. pes)	foot	impede, millipede, pedal
photo	light	photography
phobia, phobe	fear	hydrophobe, xenophobia
pneum	air, breath, spirit	pneumonia
pos, posit	place	deposit, position

pot, poss, poten (fr. ponerte)	be able	potential, possible
quaerere	ask, question, seek	inquiry, query
rog (fr. rogare)	ask	interrogate
scrib, scrip (fr. scribere)	write	scribble, script, inscribe
sent, sens (fr. sentire)	feel	sensitive, sentient
sol	alone	soloist, isolate
soph	wise	philosopher
spect (fr. spicere)	look	introspective, inspect
spir (fr. spirare)	breathe	inspiration
therm (fr. thermos)	warm	thermometer
ten (fr. tendere)	stretch	extend, tense
ten (fr. tenere)	hold	tenant
utilis	useful	utility
ven, vent (fr. venire)	come, arrive	advent, convenient
vert, vers (fr. vertere)	turn	revert, adverse
vid, vis (fr. videre)	see	supervisor, vision, provident

Vocabulary 3 (a)

1. A person who is friendly and lovable is often described as ....

2. A .... is a wise or would-be learned man.

3. Material through which light can travel is ....

4. You are .... if you are unable to perform or act.

5. An .... is a payment made yearly.

6. When an actor stands alone on a stage and speaks to himself his speech is known as a ....

7. The word ...., which now usually means to pass away or die, derives from the idea of breathing out.

8. If a bone is out of joint, or misplaced, we say it is ....

9. The transference of thoughts from one mind to another over a distance is known as ....

10. .... means to be alike in proportion, value or structure; to be in a corresponding position.

11. A person who is quarrelsome and discontented, and who complains in a questioning manner is ....

12. .... means pertaining to heat.

13. A trial hearing of an applicant for employment, especially in the case of actors and singers, is known as an ....

14. .... is the controversial art of analysing person-
    ality from handwriting.
15. If you suffer from a fear of open spaces, you suffer from
    ....

a. expire   b. translucent   c. audition   d. sophist
e. annuity   f. agoraphobia   g. querulous   h. amiable
i. thermal   j. dislocated   k. graphology   l. impotent
m. telepathy   n. soliloquy   o. homologous

Vocabulary 3 (b)

1. If you behead someone you .... him.
2. A .... person is one who will stretch a point in
   order to convince.
3. .... is the study of the physical features of the
   crust of the earth.
4. To .... is to take a complete control of the
   attention; to overcome by charm of manner and appearance.
5. A person who considers himself to be the centre of the
   universe is described as ....
6. ...., a term usually reserved for God, is
   occasionally applied to people who seem to know everything.
7. A .... is someone who holds that actions are
   right only if they are useful.
8. An .... is a statement which comes between a
   person and his intended action; a prohibition.
9. The murder of one's own father is known as ....
10. If something is made by, or results from art; if it is in
    some way artificial, we say it is ....
11. The .... is that time of year when both day and
    night are of equal length.
12. A .... is a steward or servant (someone who
    waits on you hand and foot!).
13. .... means to cause to come together; to call to
    an assembly.
14. That which has a material body is said to be ....
15. .... is leading or carrying away, usually by
    fraud or force.

a. tendentious b. artefact c. convene d. decapitate
e. corporeal f. manciple g. equinox h. captivate
i. abduction j. egocentric k. geomorphology l. omniscient
m. interdict n. utilitarian o. patricide

Vocabulary 3 (c)

1. A person who is destitute of sense or given to extremes, we call ....

2. .... is the power of projecting one's feelings into an object or person, and so reach full understanding.

3. .... means to shed light on, to make clear.

4. A .... drill is one that uses compressed air.

5. An instrument that finely measures time is a ....

6. A .... person is one who holds on, no matter what the circumstances.

7. A .... is money sent to you.

8. The science which deals with the forces exerted by air and by gaseous fluids is ....

9. The germinal matter for all living things is ....

10. When people associate as brothers, we say they ....

11. If something is .... it reminds us of death.

12. An .... may be defined as the act of placing or putting on; a burden, often unwelcome.

13. .... is when you substitute someone else for yourself in regard to asking for your legal rights.

14. .... refers to that which is deserted, laid waste, solitary, forsaken.

15. .... is a feeling of giddiness.

a. chronometer b. imposition c. subrogation d. elucidate
e. insensate f. desolation g. morbid h. vertigo
i. remittance j. fraternise k. empathy l. pneumatic
m. bioplasm n. aerodynamics o. tenacious

PART FOUR

USING YOUR EYE/BRAIN SYSTEMS
– APPLICATIONS

During the last twenty-five years, I have taught the fundamental principles of Speed and Range Reading in more than
fifty countries to students ranging from seven year old school
children to chief executives of multi-national corporations. In
every country, for every age, and no matter what the
individual's position, similar questions arise concerning the
application of the theory to the actual process of reading.
These questions include:

'I can see how you would use this for other subjects, but you
couldn't really use it for the sciences, could you?'
'You wouldn't apply Speed and Range Reading to the
appreciation of literature and poetry, would you?'
'You surely wouldn't preview a detective story!'
'On *really* difficult material, you'd *have* to read slowly,
wouldn't you?'
'Surely you wouldn't use Speed and Range Reading if you
were reading for relaxation and pleasure?'
'But I read to help me get to sleep – how can I use these
techniques to help me do that!?'

Intriguingly, the answer is that your growing knowledge of
how to Range Read can be applied to *all* the aforementioned
situations. What you have been learning and will continue to
learn throughout the pages of Speed and Range Reading is an
entire Range of reading skills from which you can pick the
appropriate individual items or combinations of items to fit
your particular reading task/goal.

From this time, every page of every book you read will be
approached slightly differently from every other page, and you
will be to the printed word as a dolphin is to water.

The chapters in Part Four give you more detailed information on advanced applications, using the new information
on your eye/brain system, and introduce you to the revolutionary new concept of the Knowledge File.

CHAPTER SEVENTEEN

THE MIND MAP ORGANIC STUDY TECHNIQUE (MMOST)

It has been said that knowledge is power. In truth power lies in the ability to assimilate, comprehend, understand, retain, recall, communicate, and the consequent ability to create new knowledge from your extant multi-dimensional mental encyclopaedia. The key to this power is learning how to learn.

Study reading is an area to which all of the information contained in Speed and Range Reading can be applied. The author has devised the Mind Map Organic Study Technique (MMOST) for this purpose. MMOST incorporates all the brain compatible skills, including Mind Mapping, the Memory Principles and Systems and the Speed and Range Reading processes. MMOST is explained in full in *Use Both Sides of Your Brain* with applications for the family in *Make the Most of Your Mind* and for business in *Harnessing the ParaBrain*.

Very briefly, the technique is divided into two parts: Preparation and Application. Each of these is divided into four parts:

I Preparation
   a) Browse
   b) Time and Amount
   c) Previous knowledge Mind Map
   d) Goals and objectives

II Application
   a) Overview
   b) Preview
   c) Inview
   d) Review

For clarification:

I Preparation

a) Browse. Use the previewing skills taught in the previous chapter to gain a 'bird's eye' view of the text.
b) Time and Amount. Set the time periods and the quantities of material to be covered in those periods. See *Use Both Sides of Your Brain*.
c) Previous Knowledge Mind Map. Using a Mind Map, search your memory for previous knowledge on the topic, thus providing an appropriate mental set.
d) Goals and Objectives. Establish clearly why you are reading the material and what you want to get out of it.

II Application

a) Overview. Do a second and 'deeper' browse, using your goals and questions to select appropriate foundation information.
b) Preview. Having established the basic structure of the information, begin to zoom in on the parts of relevance, focusing on beginnings and endings.
c) Inview. Fill in the bulk of the remaining information, building up your Mind Map, leaving difficult areas for the final stage.
d) Review. The final integration. Complete your Mind Map, solve any remaining problems, answer remaining questions and complete all your goals.

Properly applied, MMOST will transform the way you feel about the study process to a positive, motivated and energised interaction with information, and will increase your study reading efficiency and effectiveness significantly.

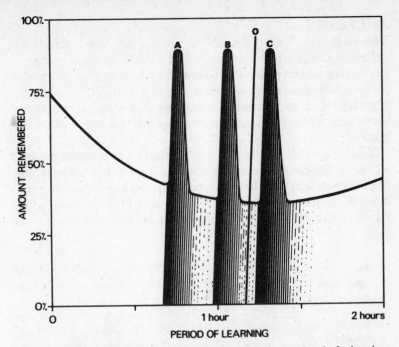

Fig. 11 Graph shows that we recall more at the beginning and end of a learning session, and also more when things are outstanding or unique (O)

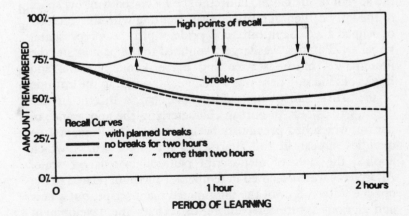

Fig. 12 Recall during period of learning with and without planned breaks

Self Test

The next Self Test selection is on slightly more difficult material, and as a result you may find a slight decrease in your performance scores. Do not be concerned about this, as most people, when reading material of this difficulty, seldom complete it at an average of more than 90 wpm. If you can score near your previous progress scores you are a phenomenon!

Your approach to this Self Test should be as follows: apply all the techniques, including advanced previewing that you have learnt previous to this chapter: quickly overview the material, looking at headings and underlined words, and rapidly establish your knowledge goals for the reading.

Start Your Timer Now

SELF TEST 7

ART – GOTHIC TO NATIONAL SCHOOLS

Gothic Art

The monumental Romanesque style was not of long duration. It disappeared with the radical change in western architecture, the advent of the Gothic church. The increased window space of the lofty cathedral replaced wall painting with the 'picture' of stained glass. Sculpture took pride of place as a representational art. Painting was largely confined to the book scale, the illumination of the service and prayer-books, missals and Books of House. There was a change, however, in the attitude of the artist (and of his wealthy patrons), a delight in fine detail, gay colour, in human character and the appearance of nature, which had previously been lacking. The Romanesque qualities appear in the altarpieces and other works which applied the style of manuscript painting to a larger scale. Altarpieces were executed in tempera, a medium related to the opaque watercolour of the illuminated manuscript, but a new and glorious future for painting came with the development of the oil medium in the 15th century. The paintings of Jan van Eyck (c. 1390–1441), who worked at Bruges, represent the climax of the detailed and beautiful Gothic style and an early perfection of oil painting.

The Renaissance

In Italy the Gothic style never took a strong hold. Church building was not drastically changed in character as it was in France and England. Artists continued to produce wall-paintings on a large scale and masterpieces were produced in constant succession from the end of the 13th century onwards. At the same time there was a change of outlook which attained its full development in the 16th century and is indicated by the word 'Renaissance'. Strictly speaking it means 'rebirth', and in art it refers to a revived interest in the classic productions of the ancient world. Thus the human figure, which the artists of the Middle Ages had shunned, once again became the artist's main subject.

This, however, was only one aspect of the Renaissance. It marked the end of the Middle Ages in other ways: in the growth of a desire for knowledge and the spirit of science. Artists began to study anatomy and the effects of light and shadow, which made their work more life-like. These studies were practised all the more freely because of a growing taste among the Italian patrons of art for other than religious subjects, for example those taken from classical myth in which the artist could group at his discretion nude and clothed figures, buildings and landscape. Botticelli is one of the great examples.

The heyday of the Renaissance is to be placed between the 15th and 16th centuries in Italy, and its great representatives are Leonardo da Vinci, Michelangelo, Raphael, Giorgione, Titian and Tintoretto. They used the perfected science of painting to create harmonies and rhythms of unsurpassed majesty and beauty.

Baroque and Rococo

Two international styles followed the Renaissance. The first is known as Baroque. It is marked by dramatic gesture and movement and was often a sort of imposing propaganda for Church and State. The work of the great Flemish painter Rubens in the 17th century provides an outstanding example of this style. It was followed in the 18th century by Rococo, a graceful and artificial mode of interior decoration, and lighter in style, exemplified for example in the paintings of the French artists, Boucher and Fragonard.

The National Schools

The observer will note that the foregoing international terms do not refer to painting alone but also to architecture and sculpture and minor forms of art and craftsmanship, such as tapestries and furniture. For a great church or the palace of a king or prince a consistent style was required. It was to some extent independent, at this princely and ecclesiastical level, from differences of race and nationality. Meanwhile, however, these differences, together with growing variations in religious beliefs and types of society, tended to produce national 'schools' of art. A 'school' implies a number of painters working in the same region whose work has some general likeness of style and outlook. Each of the main countries of Europe has, at one period or another, produced such groups of artists, whose work is not only of outstanding interest but distinct in its regional and national character.

Thus *Italy* is not only the country of the great movement called the Renaissance; it represents also a whole series of schools which grew up in the various city states into which the country was anciently divided – Florence, Siena, Parma, Venice and so on. *Florence* was astonishingly rich in great artists. They include Giotto, Fra Angelico, Botticelli, Leonardo and Michelangelo to mention only a few whose fame is universal. In Florence the 'scientific' attitude which enabled the artist to represent convincingly the weight and dignity of form in the round was cultivated to the highest degree. In this sense the Florentine genius may be called sculptural. *Venice* was the centre of another great school – here again there is a long list of famous artists, including Giovanni Bellini, Carpaccio, Giorgione, Titian, Tintoretto, Veronese and in the 18th century, Canaletto and Guardi. The Venetian School is noted for its rich colour and a more sensuous character than that of the intellectual Florentines. In the 16th century *Bologna* was the centre of a school that tried to pick out and combine the best qualities of a number of the earliest masters.

Naples in the 17th century was the centre of a rather sombre *Spanish–Italian School* of whom Ribera is typical.

The great period of the southern Netherlands, the *Flemish School* extends from the 15th to the 17th century, though it has two distinct aspects. There is first the highly detailed and mainly religious art (though including portraiture) of the early masters, van Eyck, van der Weyden and Memlinc and secondly the florid and vigorous art, varied in subject matter, which is supremely represented by Rubens.

The *Dutch School* is the product of one century, the 17th, in which the northern provinces of the Netherlands attained their independence. It is marked by a strongly national feeling and pride in its middle-class prosperity, its well kept interiors, its characteristic flat landscape, its flowers. The Dutch greatly developed portraiture, landscape and still-life and gave to art two of its greatest masters in Rembrandt and Vermeer.

French painting reaches a sustained level from the 17th to the 19th century. Centrally placed between north and south Europe, France was influenced both by Italian and Flemish art, though developing a strong individuality, to be seen in such great masters as Nicolas Poussin, Claude, Watteau, Chardin and Fragonard. A brilliant succession of painters in the 19th century, from Corot and Delacroix to Manet and the Impressionists, make this perhaps the most remarkable period of all in French painting.

The great period of *British painting* is from the early 18th to the early 19th century. Beginning with Hogarth and his pictures of social life, it comprises the achievements in portraiture of Gainsborough, Reynolds and others, and in landscape of Wilson, Gainsborough, Crome, Turner and Constable; while its school of watercolour painting was a growth without parallel elsewhere.

German art flowered in the 16th century, combining the Gothic passion for detail with an intense earnestness that did not shrink from ugliness. The great artists of this period are Matthias Grunewald, who added a masterpiece to European painting in his *Isenheim Altarpiece*, and Albrecht Durer whose engravings and drawings are among the great classics of art.

The genius of *Spain* likewise is concentrated in a few men of outstanding greatness: El Greco in the late 16th century,

Velázquez, who in achievement and influence is one of the greatest of all, and finally Goya with his keen social vision.

Stop Your Timer Now

Length of time ………. mins

SELF TEST 7 (1,300 words)

1. In the Gothic period sculpture took pride of place as a representational art.   True False

2. Gothic art produced a new attitude in the artist.   True False

3. In Italy the Gothic style never took a strong hold.   True False

4. In Italy artists produced wall paintings on a large scale and masterpieces were produced in constant succession from the end of the 13th century onwards.   True False

5. The change of outlook known as the Renaissance attained its full development in the 13th century.   True False

6. Renaissance means re-birth.   True False

7. In the Renaissance the human figure became the artist's main subject.   True False

8. The study of anatomy, light and shadow, although important, did not make Renaissance art more life-like.   True False

9. Baroque and Rococo were national styles that followed the Renaissance.   True False

10. Baroque and Rococo were, respectively, dramatic and graceful.   True False

11. Italy had only one, rather than a series of schools of art.   True False

12. The Dutch School greatly developed portraiture and landscapes.   True False

13. French painting was greatly influenced by
    Italian and Flemish art.   True   False

14. The great period of English painting lasted
    300 years.   True   False

15. German art flowered in the 16th century.   True   False

Comprehension .... Right

Percentage ....

CHAPTER EIGHTEEN

GETTING CONTROL OF YOUR NEWSPAPERS

Newspapers are one of your windows on the world, and increasingly the universe. It is possible, by understanding their nature, and approaches to them, to increase your efficiency in this arena by factors of ten.

Newspapers are so much a part of our everyday life that we seldom stop to think that they are a very recent development. Prior to the 20th century the voice of journalism was virtually non-existent so far as mass audiences were concerned. Newspapers were in the main news-sheets with very little interpretive analysis or editorial comment. There was however one note-worthy exception: *The Times*, whose critical reports of the Crimean War in 1855 have been cited as influential in the downfall of the Cabinet and the army reorganisation.

It is interesting to note that the four oldest publications surviving the upheavals of history are not more than two hundred years old:

1. Berlingske Tidende   Denmark   founded 1749
2. Yorkshire Post   England   founded 1754
3. Neue Zürcher Zeitung   Switzerland founded 1780
4. The Times   England   founded 1785

The 19th century saw a steady growth of the world press, stimulated by the introduction of the Foudrinier machine which produced paper in an endless sheet. Parallel to this development was the universal growth of communication networks and education: more information was required more rapidly, and more people were able to read. As a result many of the world's newspapers were founded between 1840 and 1900.

In the early 20th century newspapers flourished, but even now, after a fairly short existence, many are entering more

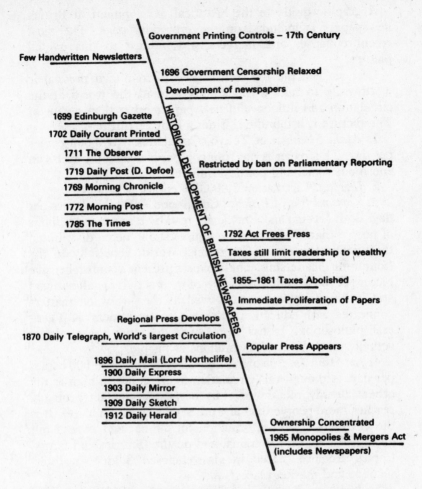

Fig. 13 Illustration showing the historical development of newspapers from the 17th century to modern times

difficult times. One reason may be the spread of television, which in many cases can give a more immediate and personal coverage of a news event.

In the western world we may well be entering a stage in which the newspaper will change its function, dealing less with immediate news and more with summaries, analyses, and comment.

A graphic guide to the historical development of British newspapers is included on the preceding page. The most recent collapses and mergers add interest to this overall picture.

Lest we become too concerned with our own press it is worthwhile to take a quick look around the world at the circulation and influence of newspapers other than our own. The picture is astounding, if not a little disturbing.

1. *Asahi Shimbun* of Tokyo. Circulation 9,000,000 copies per day. This paper is not simply a popular daily; it exerts an enormous social and political influence.

2. *Izvestia.* Circulation 8,000,000 copies per day.

3. *Komsomolskaya Pravda.* Circulation 7,000,000 copies per day. Both *Izvestia* and *Pravda* are read by many more millions of people than the circulation figures show, being distributed throughout the entire Communist world, especially to the Communist leadership. These papers present a comprehensive picture of the Communists' view of their activity in all national and international spheres, as well as their view on matters connected with education, athletics, entertainment, and general philosophy. It has been suggested that these papers actually reach *hundreds* of millions of people.

4. *Jen Minh Jih Pao* of Peking. Circulation 2,500,000 copies per day. Although this circulation figure is not so high as the others already mentioned, this newspaper in fact probably reaches more people than any other journal in the world. It is the channel of state information for China, and is read out over the radio, on the trains, and on the factories and farms. Copies are also placed in glass-enclosed holders at intersections and market places.

5. *The New York Times.* Circulation 1,000,000 copies per day. Once again the circulation figures here are misleading, for this newspaper is read mainly by the leading economic, political, and communication communities in America and much of the Western World. Its influence on opinion-leaders throughout the world is enormous.

As a matter of fact the vast majority of the world's quality press seldom exceeds a daily circulation of 400,000 copies, and this includes three of the world's most educative and analytical newspapers: *Neue Zürcher Zeitung* of Switzerland, *The Times* of England and *Le Monde* of France. As with *Jih Pao* and *The New York Times*, the circulation figures can be somewhat misleading in these cases, for the influence of these newspapers is considerable.

Approaches to Reading Newspapers

Having viewed newspapers in their international and historical setting, let us discuss briefly approaches to reading them.

1. First, it is most important to have an organised approach. Many people spend hours reading their newspaper and come away feeling no more enlightened than when they began.

2. Whatever newspaper you read, it is always helpful to decide beforehand exactly what your aim is. To assist you in this decision always rapidly preview the newspaper before you read it, selecting the various passages and articles that you wish to read more thoroughly.

3. Take a note also of the lay-out and typography, for pre-knowledge of where articles are continued, etc. saves a lot of page turning and fumbling.

4. Most people have a tendency to buy a newspaper which supports their general views – in other words they give themselves a little pat on the back every morning or evening! It can be a most interesting exercise to buy a different newspaper each day for a week, comparing and contrasting the layouts, the political bias, the approach of the reporters, the interpretation of news events, and the extent of the coverage. Try this during the coming week.

5. Newspaper reports should be checked for accuracy – I am sure that those of you who have been involved in a function or event which was reported the next day have often thought 'that's *nothing* like what happened at all!'

News is written by people who are likely to be biased or to be following a 'policy'. This 'misreporting', if we can call it that, is not necessarily intentional. Each person tends to see any given situation in a different light.

Newspaper reporters are individuals, and they may even be seeing a given event from different physical locations (being in the middle of a stampeding crowd and being in a building watching that crowd stampede are bound to produce different reports).

6. Accepting this basic and inevitable bias, we move on to the reporting of the event itself. The journalist will take down brief notes of what he wishes to report, will spend time travelling back to his typewriter, and will then reconstruct in his mind's eye the events that have taken place. Once again there will be slight and inevitable changes in emphasis which will be embellished by the words used to convey the situation.

Once the report has been written it has to be edited, and then re-edited before finally reaching the pages of the newspaper.

It can be seen that even with the most sincere of intentions, a *completely* objective report is almost impossible. Newspapers, magazines and journals should therefore be read with a far more critical eye than they usually are and what they report should be checked by news from other sources such as radio, television, and other journals.

7. This critical approach to reading must involve analytical awareness and logical thinking. Still bearing in mind all that we have said on newspapers we now move on to the next chapter where more intricate details of analysis will be covered.

8. Having assimilated steps 1 to 7, you can now take your reading of newspapers a giant leap forward by following these guidelines:

a) Decide on your main goals in reading a newspaper, and endeavour to stick to these goals as closely as possible.

b) Skim and scan articles and pages using the techniques outlined in Chapter 8.

c) Use a guide throughout (see Chapter 6).

d) As you skim and scan, mark any articles of particular interest.

e) Cut out any articles that are going to be of lasting use and interest to you.

f) Throw the rest of the newspaper out as soon as possible!

g) Use a Mind Map to record any major new information or any information which is building on a daily or weekly basis.

After you have completed a newspaper exercise, go directly to Self Test 8 – Astronomy, applying *all* the principles you have learned so far in *Speed Reading*.

SELF TEST 8

ASTRONOMY

Ancient Readings of the Sky

The study of astronomy began when Man, in his curiosity, made a significant discovery about celestial movements: they measured time. The sun fixed day and night and the sequence of the seasons. The moon and stars told the passage of the night-time hours. Calendars based on these regular cycles were devised in Babylon and Egypt long before 2500 B.C. The Egyptians divided their crop year into three seasons and always marked its beginning when the star Sirius appeared at a certain spot in the eastern sky. When Sirius showed up, it meant the Nile was about to flood. Much later the Maya of Central America used solar observations to set the time for burning off their cornfields before each year's planting, and checked their calendar against measurements of the motions of Venus.

The Emerging Celestial Patterns

It did not take early sky watchers long to realise that the arrangement of the heavens was not chaotic but had a systematic pattern. The stars hung in the sky in fixed groups, and certain groups in succession always came up in the east just before sunrise. Astronomers deduced that these constellations stretched in a belt around the circle of the heavens, and that the sun, in its apparent annual trip about the earth, always stayed within that belt. The belt constellations eventually were given names and became the 12 figures, or signs, of the zodiac. The zodiac was used, and still is, by astrologers, to foretell events in the lives of men and nations.

A different sort of celestial pattern was worked out by Greek astronomers in an attempt to explain the heavenly movements. This concept, perfected by Ptolemy, saw the sun, moon and planets moving around the earth in complex orbits. Ingenious and well-supported by the evidence of men's eyes, the Ptolemaic theory prevailed for another 13 centuries.

The Copernican Revolt

In the 16th century the work of two men helped to destroy the Ptolemaic idea of an earth-centred universe which had been accepted everywhere for 1,300 years. In 1543 Nicholas Copernicus, a brilliant Polish lawyer and astronomer, turned the old idea around by insisting that 'in the centre of everything the sun must reside . . . where he can give light to all the planets'. Although Copernicus mistakenly assumed that the planets followed perfect circle orbits, all the facts then known about the solar system were much more simply explained by his sun-centred theory than by Ptolemy's. The old ideas died hard, however, and not until the next century was the revolutionary concept accepted.

What ultimately was to be vital to the proof of the Copernican system was the work of a Danish astronomer, Tycho Brahe. Unlike Copernicus, Tycho was a measurer rather than a theoretician, and he designed astronomical instruments larger and more carefully engineered than any that had ever been used before. He built a remarkable observatory in 1576 and spent 21 years there making observations and calculations of the stars and planets with astonishing precision. Tycho himself clung to an earth-centred theory, but his research, in the hands of later scientists, helped to prove the new Copernican notions of the universe.

Enter the Telescope

When Galileo turned his primitive telescope to the sky in 1609, he saw things which men had hardly dreamed were there. He found mountains on the moon; he saw that Venus had moon-like phases which proved its sun-centred orbit. With that, the old, comforting idea of a centrally located earth was doomed. Meanwhile, in Prague, mathematician Johannes Kepler, using Tycho Brahe's measurements, calculated the planets' elliptical orbits about the sun, and upset the old concept of the circle as the typical celestial form. By observation and deduction, Kepler framed the basic laws of the solar system as it is known now, and shaped astronomy's future.

Stargazers of the East

Though science was all but blotted out in Europe during the Dark Ages, the world's accumulation of knowledge about astronomy was not lost. Both in India (from about A.D. 250) and in the Moslem world (starting four centuries later), astronomers kept on observing and calculating – and finding nothing to contradict Ptolemy's theories. Through the centuries they kept on refining all the basic instruments of naked-eye observation, such as the astrolabe for measuring stars' positions and the gnomon, or sundial, which shows the sun's movement by shadows.

Knowledge gained at observatories in Alexandria and Baghdad was carried westward to Europe and eastward to China. In India, meanwhile, astronomical efforts reached a monumental peak with the work of the 18th century astronomer Jai Singh II, who realised that the larger his observational instruments were, the more accurate they would be. He built the structures which are the biggest and perhaps the best ever made for naked-eye observations.

Astronomical Time-telling

One thing that limited medieval astronomers was the very elastic concept of time that most societies had. The day was divided conveniently enough into 12 hours, measured from the time the sun came up to when it set. The trouble was an hour in a midsummer day was a good deal longer than an hour in midwinter. Further, the only timekeepers were sundials – useless on cloudy days – and even less precise devices that operated by water power. This state of affairs was increasingly bothersome to astronomers who, by the 16th century had begun to need accurate timing for their observations.

Fortunately the metal-working and mechanical skills of Renaissance craftsmen were beginning to produce clocks for noblemen and scientists. In 1362, Giovanni de Dondi finished an astronomical clock that not only told time but also recorded the movements of the planets with an extraordinarily complicated gear train. De Dondi's masterpiece, the oldest known European mechanical clock, was the forerunner of a clockwork revolution which, in a few centuries, was producing beautiful instruments.

Length of time .... mins

SELF TEST 8 (980 words)

1. The study of astronomy began when Man
   discovered that celestial movements measured time.   True False

2. Egyptian and Mayan civilisations used
   astronomy to regulate their agriculture.   True False

3. Early sky watchers realised that the
   arrangement of the heavens was chaotic.   True False

4. The zodiac refers to the star Sirius.   True False

5. Ptolemy perfected the Greek concept of
   astronomy which saw the sun, moon and
   planets moving around the earth.   True False

6. Ptolemy's theory prevailed for 1,300 years.   True False

7. During the Dark Ages the study of
   astronomy was universally abandoned.   True False

8. One thing that limited medieval astronomers was the elastic concept of time that
   most societies had.   True False

9. In medieval times the only time-keepers
   were sun-dials.   True False

10. The first astronomical clock was made by
    the Romans.   True False

11. Nicholas Copernicus taught that the
    planets orbited the sun.   True False

12. The work of Tycho Brahe was concerned
    with astronomical measurement.   True False

13. Tycho Brahe agreed with the Copernican
    theory.   True False

14. Galileo turned his telescope to the sky in 1609.   True False

15. Johannes Kepler framed the basic laws of the solar system.   True False

Comprehension .... Right

Percentage ....

CHAPTER NINETEEN

THE LOGIC OF LOGIC

Logical awareness is always accompanied by a burst of insight. The more you understand the elegant and delightful territory of this incisive mental skill, the more easily you will bestride the domains of knowledge.

In this chapter you will be introduced to the seven major logical fallacies that regularly appear in written and spoken language. By understanding them and the nature of them, and by knowing the contexts in which they appear, you will be able to eliminate a lot of unnecessary reading, while at the same time sharpening your analytical faculties. This skill will also give you greater confidence and competence in conversation and debate.

1. Appeal to Authority

In order to convince someone of the correctness or validity of a point, people often link their statements to an authoritative figure. For example 'Bob Boot, England's top football player, uses Tuff Nuff razor blades.' This linking with an authority automatically infers that the thing linked with is, in some way, as good as the authority itself. In reality the statement gives no pertinent or interesting information about the quality of the blades at all. This kind of argument is often used in advertising.

On a more sophisticated level such an argument may appear in a form like the following, where the authority quoted *does* in fact have some relation to the linked item: 'Plato, Aristotle, Kant and Bertrand Russell all agreed on the philosophical point that I am making.' This argument sounds strong, but as in the previous fallacy its weakness lies in the fact that the *statement* itself requires consideration rather than its supporters. It is perfectly possible that each of the famous philosophers mentioned as supporting a philosophical position could have made the same mistake.

In summary, it is the *argument* and *not* the *man* which should be the basis for reaching conclusions.

2. Denigration
This is similar to Appeal to Authority, and is 'opposite'. It is often called Character Assassination and blossoms during election periods. The opponent of an idea will attack, instead of the idea, the personality of the people who are proposing that idea. The objection to this kind of argument is similar to that in Appeal to Authority: the man is not important; it is the argument itself that must be considered.

3. Emotive Language
This concerns the use of emotionally loaded words to cloud or distort judgment, preventing lucid examination of the arguments themselves. I remember well a Canadian newspaper headline which read: 'Canadian War Hero Traded for Commie Spy'. While reading the article I was expecting something far different from what the facts turned out to be: namely that the two men had been in identical positions, had very similar backgrounds, and had been caught by the respective countries in very similar circumstances. In other words a Canadian spy had been traded for a Russian spy.

Newspapers are often guilty of misleading language of this sort, and even the form of addressing notable persons may have very different associations. Think for example of the different reaction you get from a headline, which starts 'Mrs Thatcher', 'Maggie', 'The Prime Minister', 'The Iron Lady . . .'

4. Undefined Source
Many reports include phrases such as 'usually reliable sources report', 'it has been confirmed that', and 'it is a commonly known fact that'. Phrases such as these should immediately alert the reader, for they are often substitutes for saying 'there has been a rumour that' or 'we are not really sure, but'.

This same fallacy often occurs in conversations that start with some such phrase as 'we all know' or 'everybody agrees'. But *do* we all know? And *does* everybody agree? Very often not!

5. *Extrapolation*

Extrapolation means that we decide, on the basis of information presently available, what will happen in the future or in different circumstances. This is a necessary process for helping us to make decisions, but it must be understood by those making the decision that extrapolating or predicting in this manner *never* leads to certainty, only to a probability, because in the present we don't yet know perfectly the future. Many mistakes are made because people are not aware of this, especially in economics and politics. How often have economic forecasts which were given almost as gospel gone completely awry because some important factor was not properly considered, or because an unforeseeable event loomed up just after the predictions were made.

The 1970 English pre-election opinion polls provide one of the best examples of this kind of fallacy. Even with enormous staffs, political experts and competent statisticians, most of the Poll Organisations were totally wrong in predicting a Labour Party victory.

Remember then, that extrapolation or predictive argument can be useful but never certain, and that anyone who says 'these things have happened and therefore this *will* happen' is treading on very slippery ground.

6. *Argument by Analogy*

An argument by analogy is one in which B is said to be like A and therefore a sub-section of B must be like a sub-section of A. This kind of argument can appear very convincing until one realises that if B is only *like* A, then in some way it *must* be different. Arguments by analogy often fall down on exactly this point i.e. the point which makes B *different* from A.

This kind of mistake is often made in analysing war situations, in which a present war is compared to a former war, all the similarities being trotted out as evidence that what we did or did not do then we should or should not do now. The differences are often left unconsidered and it is these (different equipment, different pressures of public opinion etc.) which are in many cases the most important factors. Whole theories of historical and economic 'cycles' have been elaborated on this basis, but while they may have a limited usefulness, they are seldom reliable.

Argument by analogy is often used in conversational discussion when people casually flip off statements to the effect 'well, such and such is like that, so the following *must* be true'. The 'following', as we have seen, need *not*, necessarily be true.

This is an insidious form of argument, so be on the lookout.

7. *Misuse of Statistics*

People often say 'you can prove anything by statistics'. What they are saying in effect is that if you are not aware of all the considerations that go into a statistical statement, you can be easily mislead.

Let me give two examples of common misrepresentations which will indicate how statistics can be juggled.

The first is the fallacy of the 'average'. In this form of statement items are added together, and the total number is then divided by the number of items. Popular surveys often make this kind of error when they conclude that the average person feels a certain way about a certain topic. To illustrate just how wrong this kind of statement can be let us construct an hypothetical situation in which a country is almost at civil war over a moral question. If we assign numbers from one to a hundred for the strength with which a person aligns himself with one of the sides, we find that half the country is *completely* opposed, each person having a score of zero, while the other half is *completely* in favour, each person having a score of one hundred. A naive analysis of these statistics might lead someone to say that the average person in the country we are discussing scored fifty, which is representative of someone who does not really care.

In fact, as we have demonstrated, there is *no* average person in our made-up country, and half the population is ready to leap at the throats of the other half.

A second statistical misrepresentation is graphic. The shape and dimensions of graphs are changed to make the same situation look quite different. Rather than explaining this in detail I have included two graphs on the following page which show a progress during a ten year period. You will see how different they appear.

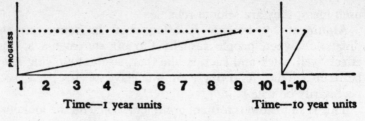

Fig. 14 Statistical misrepresentation in graphics

There are of course other logical fallacies, but the ones covered here are among the most important, and continually arise in newspapers and magazines as well as in mass media reporting, comment, and, as previously mentioned, the political arena. They tend to arise similarly in conversation, and hunting them out can be a challenging and rewarding experience.

Near the end of Chapter 18 it was recommended that you read a number of different newspapers, bringing to bear on them all your critical abilities. Now that you have more weaponry, go quickly through them again noting in just how many places the various fallacies arise. Similarly, listen for (and note outstanding ones) the various logical fallacies in newspaper and political debates. To begin with you will find that hunting them down is a little difficult, but as you persevere your facility will increase considerably and your reading will not only be more enjoyable but will be more useful because you will have become a sifter, analyser and integrator rather than a sponge.

CHAPTER TWENTY

GETTING THE FULL VALUE FROM LITERATURE AND POETRY

Why read poetry and literature?
Because the great minds of history have left us, in
them, easy stepping stones into the worlds of
imagination, fantasy, ideas, philosophy, laughter
and adventure; because by reading them you add
to your own knowledge and your own historical
and cultural data banks; because they are food for
your soul.

The points to be discussed in this chapter will encourage you to take a wider interest in this form of writing, and subsequently to read more widely about the approaches to its appreciation.

To make the discussion more comprehensible I shall discuss separately the following aspects of the novel as an art: plot, theme, philosophy, stand-point, character development, mood and atmosphere, setting, imagery, symbolism, and language.

The more you understand of each of these elements, the more your speed and comprehension in reading fiction will benefit. If you are studying literature in school or university, the following aspects are invaluable as guide posts in analysis. These guide-post areas provide ideal main branches for your Mind Map notes, and as headings in essays and examinations.

The Elements of Literature
Plot
Plot is the basic structure of events in the novel; the storyline, if you wish. It may range from a relatively minor role in primarily descriptive writing to a major role in the better *Who-Done-Its* and mystery novels.

Theme

The theme is what the plot is about. For example in *The Forsyte Sage*, a series of novels which deal with the history of a Victorian family, the theme might variously be considered to be capitalism versus creativity, conservatism versus liberalism, conformity versus individuality or riches versus poverty. Sub-themes which run parallel to the main one often occur in novels. Sub-themes often concern minor love affairs and secondary characters.

Philosophy

Philosophy is the system of ideas governing the universe of the work, and can often be thought of as the author's comment on the themes with which the book deals. Novelists known for the philosophical content in their novels include Dostoevsky, Sartre and Thomas Mann.

Stand-Point

Stand-point is *not* necessarily the author's point of view or personal feeling about what he is writing but is more often the physical stand-point from which the events described are seen. The author may, for instance, be all-knowing, standing apart and viewing the past, present and future of the event he is describing (Henry James advocated abandoning this device as he felt it clouded true representation).

In opposition to this omniscient point of view, the author may place himself in the first person (the author becomes the 'I' of the book) as in Hammond Innes' adventure stories and *Lolita* by Nabokov.

Character Development

Character development concerns the changes the persons in the story undergo. It may range from one extreme like Fleming's James Bond, who remains completely unchanged throughout his series, to Etienne in Zola's *Germinal* who develops from a rebellious youth into a mature and dedicated man. Character development can also refer to the style with which the author presents, by description of physical or mental character, movement, etc.

Mood and Atmosphere

These two terms refer to the manner in which the author evokes reality or unreality and the emotional response of the reader. Some people prefer to use only one of these terms, although they can be distinguished when placed together: mood can be described as the reaction felt by the individual to the atmosphere of a piece of writing, which can be defined as the environment. For example, the atmosphere in Poe's stories might be described as morbid and menacing, while the mood of his readers might vary from depressed to exhilarated.

Setting

Setting refers to the physical locale and the time period in which the events take place. Because the setting is usually quite apparent, its importance is often underestimated – yet the slightest variations in time and place are often very significant. Recently the setting has become even more important because of its close links with symbolism.

Imagery

Imagery is often described as the use of simile and metaphor in language, meaning that items and events are described in creative or fanciful language. The root word 'image' is perhaps most useful in coming to an understanding of this term. Examples: Sir Walter Scott, in *The Heart of Midlothian*, described Edinburgh as 'the pulsating heart core of the Scottish scene'; and Dickens, in *The Tale of Two Cities* when describing the uncovering of a prisoner buried alive for eighteen years uses images of death and burial – heavy wreaths, cadaverous colours and emaciated heads and figures. Darkness and shadows prevail.

Symbolism

Simply explained, symbolism means that one thing stands for or represents another. Throughout much of literary history the Earth, for example, has symbolised fertility and reproduction.

Since the theories of Freud, symbolism has become an increasingly important factor in literature with a new emphasis on the sexual. Any jutting object such as a gun or tree is used to symbolise the male sex organs, and any circular or hollow object such as a box or a circular pond is used to symbolise the female sex organs. An excellent example of symbolism can be found in *The Tale of Two Cities*, when a cask of red wine is spilt. The populace drink the muddy dregs with relish, signifying the hungry despair which later results in the spilling of real blood in the French Revolution. In D. H. Lawrence's *The Fox* the frozen waste in which two women live symbolises their frigidity which is attacked by the male character who eliminates a fox (symbolising the general male 'threat'). His killing of the fox with his gun places him in the dominant male role.

Symbolism may be much more obscure than in these examples, and the reader who understands it will often be one of the very few who grasps the full meaning of much of great literature.

Language

Authors' use of language varies from the tough masculine style of Hemingway to the flowing and poetic language of Nabokov. The language an author uses is always revealing, and if you pay careful attention to it you will often gain far deeper insight into the shades of meaning and mood within the work.

In discussing aspects of style in the novel I have dealt with each item separately, but should like to make clear that each is inseparably linked to all the others. The very setting of a story, for example, may be symbolic – and so it is with the other aspects. When you read literature, always try to be aware of the intricate interlacings and interrelationships of the aspects that have been discussed.

Poetry

Many people insist that poetry should be read very slowly. Our talking speed is about 200 words a minute, but many of us tend to read poetry at less than 100. Actually this hinders a proper appreciation, for a slow, plodding trudge through a poem effectively destroys the natural rhythm, and in consequence conceals much of the meaning from the reader. In schools this problem is made worse by teachers who fail to correct students when they read each line as though the meaning lay at the end. This is often simply not the case. Sophisticated poets let their meaning flow *through* the lines.

The best approach to the reading of poetry is as follows:

1. A very rapid preview enabling you to find out roughly what the poem is about and where it leads.

2. A second rapid but more thorough reading to get a more accurate idea of the way in which the lines relate to each other and the way in which the thought and rhythm interlink and progress.

3. A leisurely ramble through the poem concentrating on areas of particular interest.

4. Reading aloud.

Fig. 15 Sometimes it is a good idea to simply go to a restful spot and lose yourself in a writer's world

In the final analysis speed is often irrelevant in an approach to literature and poetry – the situation becoming more like listening to music or appreciating art. One does not listen to Beethoven's 5th Symphony once and disregard it with the triumphant claim 'Well, I've done that at an average speed of 33 rpm!'

When reading literature and poetry, bring to bear all your knowledge and judgment, and if you feel that it is the kind of writing you wish to treasure forever, forget about speeding through it and reserve it for those occasions when time is not so pressing.

Self Test 9 is the History of Communications. From now on there is no need for you to apply the full study technique in the Self Tests. Your approach should be to apply *whatever* seems most appropriate from all that you have learned. In other words, you should now begin to make your own decisions about the way in which you will tackle any given material.

As you have done in the previous Self Tests, continue with your endeavour to improve on previous performances.

Start Your Timer Now

SELF TEST 9
THE HISTORY OF COMMUNICATIONS

Considering the importance of language in the development of human society, it is astonishing to find how little is known about its origins. Writing, which by definition is a lasting record, occurred quite late in human history, but speech, which is by nature evanescent, may have arisen tens of thousands of years before writing first appeared. Who knows what language, if any, was spoken by paleolithic man, he whose bones, whose tools, whose paintings on the walls of caves have survived, but not his speech? The absence of any real evidence for the origin of human speech has opened the subject up to endless speculation. There were always those, of course, who held that speech was divinely revealed to Man, a gift from God. Others more logical but no less wide of the mark – including Democritus, Locke, Condillac, and Adam Smith – held that speech was adopted by Mankind in convention; in other words that it might be looked upon as an artificial creation legislated, so to speak, into existence.

From the nineteenth century onward, research into the origins of speech increased in quantity, seriousness, and intensity – but the results were as meagre as ever. Among recent scholars several alternative theories have arisen and have been given colourful names which should not detract from their serious intent. There is, for instance, the 'bow-wow' theory, which holds that human words first arose from imitations of natural sounds such as the barking of a dog. Or the 'pooh-pooh' theory, that speech began with exclamations of fear, pain, pleasure, and the like, and its close relative the 'yo-he-ho' theory, that it started with grunts of physical exertion, or the 'sing-song' theory, holding that primitive chants opened the way to speech. The Soviet scholar Marr considers that articulate speech began as an accompaniment to communication by gesture. And he bases all variations and combinations in subsequent speech on only four primitive sounds originally used with these gestures – sol, ber, yon, and rok. Other linguists believe that speech appears only when, as with children, a person's mental activity attains a certain level of development.

All of this admirable scholarship does little to clarify the actual origin of language. In fact, most of it is just as speculative as the persistent legend that the first and original language was the 'language of the birds'. This bizarre idea crops up among the ancient Egyptians, among the Incas of South America, and in the stories of Orpheus, Siegfried and St. Francis of Assisi. It was quite seriously discussed by the medieval alchemist Fulcanelli, who wrote, 'Those rare writers who have spoken of the "language of the birds" accord it first place in the origins of speech. They say that it goes back to Adam, who used it to impose under God's will suitable names designed to define the characteristics of the people and things of creation.'

The idea that there must have been *some* original language is as persistent as the legend of the 'language of the birds'. Up to the end of the seventeenth century, Hebrew, the language of divine revelation, was held to be the original language of humanity. Leibnitz protested vigorously against this view, and gradually emphasis shifted from a search for the single original language to the fact, which was becoming increasingly obvious, that there were groups, or families, of languages. In attempting to unravel the relationships that linked the various tongues scholars began to develop a new tool for the study of the origin and diffusion of languages. Historical and comparative linguistics, especially as applied to the problem of the

Indo-European group of languages in the nineteenth century, began to provide a far sounder and more scientific basis for the study of language in general.

Years of careful and devoted scholarship have built up a picture of the world's languages, living and dead, which is almost frightening in its complexity. It is estimated that at the present time there are some 3,000 languages currently in use. In Europe alone scholars count 120. Then there are the dead languages, including Sumerian, Sanskrit, Avestan, Latin, Phoenician, Scythian, Iberian, and the rest. Altogether, it seems that almost 4,000 languages have disappeared during the course of human, and thus lingual, evolution. A strange example is the Etruscan, which can be read because it was written in a Greek script, but understood very little or not at all because its syntax differs from that of every known language.

And all these languages, living and dead – except for a few, such as the Baswue and the Japanese Ainu, which so far have defied classification – are complexly interrelated, through common origins, similar structure, word roots, and word sounds, thus falling into family groups, and subdivisions of these groups, some enormous, some quite insignificant. The largest overall groupings are the African, Semitic-Hamitic, Indo-European, Sino-Tibetan, Japanese-Korean, Ural-Altaic Austronesian, North American Indian, and South American Indian. To these, many other groups and subgroups may be added ad infinitum: the Caucasian, the Dravidian, the Finno-Ugrian, 26 smaller families from North America, including Eskimo, Algonquin, Uto-Aztec and Iroquois, 20 from Central America including Mayan and Zapotecan, and 77 from South America and the West Indies, including Arawak, Carib, and Chibcha. The count for the classification of all the Indian languages is still in an embryonic state.

Of these so-called 'families' of languages, some may be spoken by mere thousands of people, whereas the Sino-Tibetan languages of southeastern Asia are spoken by well over 600 million people, and the Indo-Iranian languages by some 400 million. Yet the latter is merely one subgroup of the great Indo-European, or Aryan, family of lanugages, which includes numerous other subgroups, such as the Germanic,

Romance, Slavic, and lesser units like the Greek, Albanian, and Armenian.

The Indo-European family of languages, now used by about half of the world's population, is supposed to have stemmed from a small, compact area – variously located from the Iranian plateau through Central Europe to the Baltic – whose inhabitants migrated south and westwards before 2000 B.C., spreading the basic structure of their language to many diverse areas. Much later, Latin, a minor Indo-European dialect centred near the mouth of the Tiber River, spread by conquest over most of Europe and the Mediterranean. Offshoots of Latin and of the Germanic subgroup of the Indo-European family – French, Spanish, and English – have now travelled around the world. Yet the close relationships of the many widespread branches of the Indo-European is nevertheless still quite clear. Travellers to Iran, for instance, are astonished to find that such basic words as 'mother' and 'father' are almost the same as in English.

Such a picture of languages and language groups growing and dying, evolving, splitting, competing, ever active and ever changing, seems utterly confusing until it is remembered that language is merely an expression of human society. Languages, like cultures, nations, and civilisations, tend to disintegrate into local groupings unless there is a strong centralising influence to enforce unity and growth. The Romans spread Latin around the known world, but when the Roman Empire broke up, Latin, too, diverged into the various Romance languages we know today. Languages follow social, political, economic, and religious trends. Dying languages, for instance, have been revived for political reasons – as in Ireland and Israel. Even within a given language area, differences in dialect, usage, and vocabulary will reflect the fine shadings of class differences, of the differences between young and old, and between professions.

Length of time .... mins

SELF TEST 9 (1,270 words)

1. Astonishingly little is known about the origins of language.   True False

2. Writing occurred early in human history.   True False

3. Democritus, Locke, Condillac and Adam Smith saw 'speech' as an artificial creation.   True False

4. The pooh-pooh theory holds that human words first arose from imitations of natural sounds such as the barking of a dog.   True False

5. Much of the scholarship and theoretical suggestion on language does little to clarify its origin.   True False

6. Research into language is called 'hieroglyphics'.   True False

7. Until the 17th century the original language of mankind was thought to be Hebrew.   True False

8. Leibnitz supported the theory that Hebrew was the original language of mankind.   True False

9. Historical and comparative linguistics provided a sounder and more scientific basis for the study of language.   True False

10. In Europe 120 languages are current.   True False

11. The Baswue and the Japanese Ainu language were among those that were easy to classify.   True False

12. The Indo-European group of languages are spoken by half the world's population.   True False

13. Latin was a minor Indo-European dialect centred near the mouth of the Tiber river.   True   False

14. The relationship of the widespread branches of the Indo-European language is now not very clear.   True   False

15. Languages follow social, political, economic and religious trends.   True   False

Comprehension .... Right

Percentage ....

CHAPTER TWENTY-ONE

CREATING YOUR KNOWLEDGE FILE – YOUR BRAIN'S EXTERNAL DATA BANK

Knowledge is one thing; organised knowledge is a billion things!

At this stage of *Speed Reading*, you are ready and able to create your own Knowledge Files – a 'data garden' which you tend and nurture using the skills you have learnt.

The Knowledge File

Your Knowledge File should take the form of a standard loose-leaf ring binder, ideally large enough to take 500 pages. Within this should be dividers for each of your major areas of interest. You can discover these easily by doing a quick Mind Map, the centre of which is an image of yourself with an enquiring mind. Quickly Mind Map all those areas of knowledge that are of major interest to you, and you will find the main branches of your Mind Map will provide an adequate first definition of your areas.

Keeping Your Knowledge File

Once you have defined your major areas of interest, the next stage is to save up the information in each section. This you do by filing any summary Mind Maps you might have made during your reading and study in each of the areas, and especially by storing those articles you will have selected when reading your newspapers and magazines (see Chapter 18).

Tending Your Knowledge File

It is important to manage your time, Knowledge File and yourself elegantly and effectively. One way to do this is to select appropriate articles and information over a period of a month in one given interest area, and to consider that information as a book or booklet. At the end of a month, read it *as a book*. Combine Range Reading skills and the Mind

Map Organic Study Technique, and your reading effectiveness will be increased in a number of ways: first, you'll have a similarly-directed mental set while reading *every* article and piece of information, secondly you will be obtaining the Gestalt of all the information together, and thirdly many 'different' articles appearing during the same time tend to repeat similar information – you can therefore save an enormous amount of time by skimming over repetitive areas.

Mind Mapping Your Knowledge File Knowledge
As you read your Knowledge File in these ways, keep growing on-going Mind Map summaries of your expanding knowledge. This constant review and integration will guarantee you not only a great understanding, but also a much more retentive memory. This combination will lead you to the next stage:

The Master Mind Map
On your Master Mind Map you summarise all the major elements of any given area of knowledge. It is the 'Master Code' by which your brain can access its data banks. As your Master Mind Map grows, the boundaries of it will begin to link with other subjects, and what you already know increasingly becomes an associational aid to knowing even more. The different areas of interest will begin to interlace more intricately, and you will reach the stage of a comprehensive General Knowledge. As you do so, you will realise that the more you know, the more *easy* it is to know more!

A Shrinking Knowledge File?!
Myself and those of my students who have developed Knowledge Files and Master Mind Maps have found an extraordinary event occurring after two to five years – our knowledge files actually began to shrink.

This is because, as your base of knowledge grows, so does your ability to remember and integrate additional knowledge.

As you continue to nurture your Knowledge File, you find that many of your once 'important' articles can be discarded. Your knowledge file then becomes a condensed, elegant and timeless summary of the essences of your particular interests. You will have become a Master Learner.

CHAPTER TWENTY-TWO

WHAT YOU HAVE ACCOMPLISHED SO FAR – YOUR EXTRAORDINARY POSSIBILITIES FOR THE FUTURE

Create yourself. You create the Future.

Your reading course is nearing the end of its first stage. This stage is the completion of the book. Your next stages will include your subsequent reviews of *Speed Reading*, your continuing practice of the new skills you have discovered, and the compilation of your Mind Maps of all the books you read from now on and which you wish to remember.

At this stage it would be useful for us quickly to review what you have done, and to set you correctly on your future path.

In Part I reading was defined and related to how the eye and brain actually function. Common problems were seen in a new light with brain compatible solutions given.

You were introduced also to the first of the Self Tests. As mentioned in the Preface, these tests dealt with the basic areas of human knowledge, and they were by no means easy. They represent the meatiest kind of material you are likely to be faced with in your general reading and also perhaps in your study reading. If you have managed to improve your word-per-minute score on these tests, you have done well. (Many books on speed reading have 'improvement tests' that use either very easy material or material only a few paragraphs long. In either case the 'excellent' scores from such tests are not valid, for they do not test you thoroughly or in a reading situation similar to normal reading.)

I hope that the Self Tests have not only enabled you to gauge your progress, but have also encouraged you to read more widely. *All* subjects are interesting once you know how to approach them.

In Part II information on the eye and the brain was related

to special skills that build reading speed, comprehension and memory.

As the book progressed you were introduced to techniques including skimming and scanning that enabled you to get an over-view of your reading material. This was eventually combined with the concept of previewing and further supported by a discussion of the way in which paragraphs are structured and material is presented. Critical analysis and logic are added to your artillery.

By the time you were well into the book, the vocabulary chapters had been introduced and you were on the way to becoming a reader who was aware not only of the general background and basic theory in the field, but who was also consciously improving the basic material with which one deals: the words themselves.

In Part IV the application of this information and skill building to all relevant areas, such as study, newspapers, logical thinking, literature and poetry as well as creating a Knowledge File was explained.

It is obvious that these techniques are best taught under direct instructor supervision, such as is given at Buzan Centres around the world. The material you have been given in this book lays the perfect groundwork for such courses.

Your continuing success in all fields of speed reading depends on your personal decision to continue the course you have begun, and on the capacity of your brain to read, assimilate, comprehend, recall, communicate and create abilities which we know approach the infinite. Your success is therefore guaranteed.

Your final reading test will give you further information on your amazing brain. While reading it, bring to bear *all* the relevant knowledge you have gained from *Speed Reading*, and do everything you can to surpass your previous performances. As you read *The Enchanted Loom – Your Brain*, you will realise that you are even more amazing than the amazing you have now begun to think you are.

Bon voyage!

SELF TEST 10

THE ENCHANTED LOOM — YOUR BRAIN

The human brain and its potential

The human brain is an enchanted loom where millions of flashing shuttles weave a dissolving pattern, always a meaningful pattern, though never an abiding one. It is as if the Milky Way entered upon some cosmic dance.

Sir Charles Sherrington

To compare the brain with a galaxy is in fact a modest analogy. Every intact person on our planet carries around his three-and-a-half-pound mass of tissue without giving much thought to it; but every normal brain is capable of making more patterned inter-connections than there are atoms in the universe.

The brain is composed of about ten billion nerve cells and each one is capable of being involved in a vast series of complex connections thousands of times every second. At a mathematical level alone, the complexity is astounding. There are ten billion neurons in the brain and each one has a potential of connections of 10^{28}. In more comprehensible terms, it means that if the theoretical number of potential connections in your brain were to be written out, we would get a figure beginning with 1 and followed by about ten million miles of noughts.

All this is potential, of course, and, despite the manifold detailed discoveries of neurophysiology, many of which are dealt with in this book*, it is your brain's potential which is most exciting. It is undisputed that we all underuse our brains – if we do not actually abuse them. This is hardly surprising. Few of us will ever see a human brain. Those who have do not describe it as a particularly remarkable sight. It is understandable that a concert pianist or a carpenter should

---

*See book lists at beginning and end of this book.

value his hands above all, that a painter should cherish his eyes, that a runner should be most concerned about his legs. But hands are as useless without a brain as the piano itself without a player. The brain's potential has been largely underestimated just because of its omnipresence. It is involved in all we do, in everything that happens to us, and so we note that which is different in each experience, overlooking that without which nothing is possible for us.

We have been too much concerned with differences rather than potential in another, more important, sense. Since we have known that such things as brains existed we have devoted most of our efforts not to improving them but to devising systems to demonstrate the differences between them. This applies not only in education, where pass or fail is the ultimate criterion, but in every aspect of our lives. We are American or Chinese, scholar or peasant, artist or scientist. These distinctions exist, of course, and it would be foolish to dismiss them completely. But the inherent ability of each brain in its own right is important too. In every head is a formidable powerhouse, a compact, efficient organ whose capacity seems to expand further towards infinity the more we learn of it.

John Rader Platt expressed this view:

> If this property of complexity could somehow be trans-formed into visible brightness so that it would stand forth more clearly to our senses, the biological world would become a walking field of light compared to the physical world. The sun with its great eruptions would fade to a pale simplicity compared to a rose bush, an earthworm would be a beacon, a dog would be a city of light, and human beings would stand out like blazing suns of complexity, flashing bursts of meaning to each other through the dull night of the physical world between. We would hurt each other's eyes. Look at the haloed heads of your rare and complex companions. Is it not so?

The basis of this 'property of complexity' is the nerve cell – the neuron. Even those which are microscopically small are in themselves remarkably complex. Neurons differ from most other cells in that they are a more complicated shape and have many branching prolongations which can connect with each other to transmit nerve impulses. Throughout the nervous system the neurons vary tremendously in size. Some, running from the toes or the fingers into the spinal cord, can be as much as a metre in length. Others, in the cerebral cortex for example, are more than a thousand times smaller.

Everything we do, from moving a muscle to thinking great thoughts, involves intricate neuronal functioning. Whatever the activity, however, the process is similar and is founded on the excitation of the neuron. The process consists of electro-chemical signals being passed from one neuron to another: not just singly or slowly but in rapid, multiple waves of communication. Each neuron has a main body which contains specific chemical and genetic information and an axon which conducts the vital nerve impulses. It will also have a variable number of branching dendrites. These are the receivers of the impulses or information, either directly from a sense organ or, more commonly, from other neurons in the tapestry of connections.

The precise location of the transmission of the impulse from one neuron to another is your synapse where the information 'flows' across a microscopic gap not unlike the spark plug gap or the distributor points in the internal combustion engine. The physics and chemistry of this process are immensely intricate. In the synapse chemical substances are released which enable the electrical impulses to be transmitted and the synapse has a threshold which affects how readily the impulse is accepted. In familiar or reflex activity the threshold is lower so that the circuit operates more readily. A higher threshold means that the signal is more difficult to transmit.

An impulse from a single neuron causes activation in the synapses it forms with others and even the simplest mental or physical process involves certainly hundreds of neurons receiving and transmitting impulses in complex cascading waves of communication and co-operation. A hundred thousand neuronal 'messages' a second is commonplace.

Everything we do and experience, therefore, involves this intricate bio-electrical process – from playing tennis to paying the bills. This is not as perplexing as it might seem. We know that the eyes do not in themselves see: they are merely lenses. The ears do not in themselves hear: they are, so to speak, microphones. When we watch a cricket match on television we do not see the players themselves but electronic representations of them on the picture tube. What is between the cat you see in the flesh and your brain's image of the cat is a series of neurophysiological processes, just as there is a series of electronic processes between the actual cricket match and the image you see on television.

Our brains are, almost literally, everything. We can give more to them and in turn, and in addition, they can give to us. The brain is our secret, silent weapon. If we can just begin to use more of its power, we will indeed see a light that will hurt, but astonish, our eyes. To again quote John Rader Platt:

> Many of our most sensitive spirits today still see Man as the anti-hero; the helpless victim of weapons and wars, of governments and mechanisms and soul-destroying organisations and computers – as indeed he is. But in the midst of this man-made and inhuman entropy, like a fourth law of Man, there grows up, even in the laboratories, a realisation that Man is also mysterious and elusive, self-determining and perpetual. A lighthouse of complexity and the organising child of the universe. One equipped and provided for to stand and choose and act and control and be.

Stop Your Timer Now

Length of time .... mins

SELF TEST 10 (1,400 words)

1. Sir Charles Sherrington compared your brain to the Milky Way galaxy entering upon a cosmic dance.   True   False

2. Your brain weighs between 5 and 7lbs.   True   False

3. Your brain is composed of one billion nerve cells.   True   False

4. Most people use their brain's potential well.   True   False

5. John Rader Platt expressed the view that if the property of your brain's complexity could be transformed into visible brightness it would be brighter than the physical world as we know it.   True   False

6. The basis of your brain's 'property of complexity' is the neuron – the nerve cell.   True   False

7. Throughout your nervous system most neurons are the same size.   True   False

8. Some neurons can be as much as a metre in length.   True   False

9. Whatever you do, from moving a muscle to thinking great thoughts, involves a similar process that is founded on the excitation of your brain cell (neuron).   True   False

10. This process consists of signals being passed from one neuron to another, in rapid, multiple waves of communication.   True   False

11. The location of the transmission of the impulse from one neuron to another is your synapse.   True   False

12. The physics and chemistry of this process are extremely simple.   True   False

13. For your brain to send 100,000 neuronal messages a second is commonplace.   True   False

14. The eyes are not merely lenses, they actually see.   True   False

15. John Rader Platt stated that the fourth law of Man concerned our realisation that Man is mysterious and elusive, self-determining and perpetual.   True   False

Comprehension .... Right

Percentage ....

SELF TEST ANSWERS

Self Test 1
1.F 2.F 3.T 4.F 5.T 6.F 7.F 8.T 9.T 10.T 11.T 12.F 13.T 14.F 15.T

Self Test 2
1.F 2.T 3.F 4.F 5.F 6.F 7.T 8.F 9.F 10.T 11.F 12.F 13.F 14.F 15.F

Self Test 3
1.T 2.F 3.F 4.F 5.T 6.T 7.F 8.F 9.F 10.T 11.F 12.F 13.T 14.F 15.T

Self Test 4
1.F 2.T 3.T 4.T 5.F 6.F 7.T 8.T 9.F 10.T 11.T 12.T 13.F 14.T 15.F

Self Test 5
1.T 2.T 3.F 4.F 5.T 6.T 7.T 8.F 9.F 10.T 11.F 12.F 13.T 14.F 15.F

Self Test 6
1.T 2.T 3.F 4.T 5.T 6.F 7.T 8.F 9.F 10.F 11.T 12.T 13.F 14.F 15.T

Self Test 7
1.T 2.T 3.T 4.T 5.F 6.T 7.T 8.F 9.F 10.T 11.F 12.T 13.T 14.F 15.T

Self Test 8
1.T 2.T 3.F 4.F 5.T 6.T 7.F 8.T 9.T 10.F 11.T 12.T 13.F 14.T 15.T

Self Test 9
1.T 2.F 3.T 4.F 5.T 6.F 7.T 8.F 9.T 10.T 11.F 12.T 13.T 14.F 15.T

Self Test 10
1.T 2.F 3.F 4.F 5.T 6.T 7.F 8.T 9.T 10.T 11.T 12.F 13.T 14.F 15.T

VOCABULARY EXERCISE ANSWERS

Chapter 14
Exercise 1 (a)
1.l 2.e 3.m 4.f 5.n 6.g 7.o 8.d 9.k 10.c 11.j 12.b 13.i 14.a 15.h

Exercise 1 (b)
1.e 2.i 3.d 4.n 5.j 6.f 7.k 8.c 9.a 10.l 11.g 12.o 13.m 14.h 15.b

Exercise 1 (c)
1.h 2.a 3.o 4.b 5.k 6.c 7.n 8.d 9.l 10.m 11.g 12.j 13.f 14.i 15.e

Chapter 15
Exercise 2 (a)
1.f 2.l 3.k 4.i 5.e 6.h 7.d 8.n 9.m 10.a 11.j 12.b 13.g 14.c 15.o

Exercise 2 (b)
1.o 2.h 3.a 4.b 5.m 6.n 7.f 8.d 9.j 10.f 11.g 12.k 13.i 14.l 15.c

Exercise 2 (c)
1.o 2.f 3.c 4.n 5.m 6.i 7.k 8.a 9.j 10.l 11.b 12.e 13.g 14.d 15.h

Chapter 16
Exercise 3 (a)
1.h 2.d 3.b 4.l 5.e 6.n 7.a 8.j 9.m 10.o 11.g 12.i 13.c 14.k 15.f

Exercise 3 (b)
1.d 2.a 3.k 4.h 5.j 6.l 7.n 8.m 9.o 10.b 11.g 12.f 13.c 14.e 15.i

Exercise 3 (c)
1.e 2.k 3.d 4.l 5.a 6.o 7.i 8.n 9.m 10.j 11.g 12.b 13.c 14.f 15.h

APPENDIX

As you approach the end of *Speed Reading*, I hope that you will be realising that it is not the end but the real beginning. With the physical beauty and complexity of your brain, and its enormous intellectual and emotional powers, with your ability to absorb information and to manage the memorisation of that information, and with the new techniques for allowing your brain to express and organise itself in matters which are more comprehensively attuned to the way you function, reading, studying, learning, and life in general should become what they can be: delightful and flowing processes that bring not pain and frustration but pleasure and fulfilment.

Anyone interested in courses, products, or further reading dealing with the subject covered in *Speed Reading* can contact:

Buzan Centres (800) **Y MIND MAP**
415 Federal Highway FAX: (407) 845-3210
Lake Park, FL 33403
(407) 881-0188

1. THE BRAIN CLUB

The Brain Club is an international organisation designed to help you increase your mental, physical, and spiritual awareness. This is done by waking that sleeping giant, your Brain, and teaching you how to access its vast intelligences, first by Learning How to Learn and then by developing specific skills in areas that you choose.

You can do this by studying in your own home, or meeting regularly with others who also wish to expand their vast range of mental skills as outlined in *Speed Reading*.

Join these 'mental gymnasiums' and improve the following skill areas:

a Memorising
b Range/Speed Reading
c Mind Mapping
d Creative Thinking
e Learning and Studying
f IQ
g Mathematics
h The Arts
i Physical performance

j Vocabulary Building/Language Learning
k Communicating
l Personality Development
m Game skills
n Specialist skills

Each skill area within The Brain Club will be graded and certificates awarded as you reach advancing levels of competence. For details about The Brain Club, please contact The Buzan Centre, Inc.

2. PRODUCTS

The Buzan Centre offers many products useful for expanding the brain's potential.

Audiotapes

Supercreativity and Mind Mapping—a comprehensive introduction to the workings of your brain, and the theory and use of Mind Mapping (with manualette by Tony Buzan).

Make the Most of Your Mind—based on the book of the same name.

Learning and Memory—an interview with Tony Buzan, produced by *Psychology Today* magazine.

Videotapes

Improving Mental Performance—Buzan Business Training—three complete business training courses emphasising the application of Mind Mapping, Memory and Information Management to business.

The Enchanted Loom—documentary on the brain featuring interviews with the world's major contributors to the field, devised and presented by Tony Buzan.

Developing Family Genius—complete video series based in *Use Both Sides of Your Brain* and *Make the Most of Your Mind*, which guides the family through the latest information on the brain and learning how to learn.

Posters

'Body and Soul' poster—a limited edition poster depicting, in a surrealist manner, the principles taught by Tony Buzan. This beautiful

picture is called 'Body and Soul' and each numbered copy is signed by the Swedish artist Ulf Ekberg.

Mind Map Kits

Specially designed Mind Map pads, with pens and highlighters.

Master Your Memory Matrix 0-10,000 (SEM^3)

Laminated 0–99 and 100 to 10,000 Matrix (SEM^3) plus full instructions to assist the *Master Your Memory Reader*.

To order any of these products, please contact The Buzan Centre, Inc.

3. THE UNIVERSAL PERSONAL ORGANISER (UPO)

This *new* and *unique* approach to time and self management is a diary system, based on the techniques created and taught by Tony Buzan.

The Universal Personal Organiser is a living system that grows with you, and that provides a comprehensive perspective on your life, your desires, and your business and family functions.

The Universal Personal Organiser is the first diary system to use the principles that Leonardo da Vinci discovered in the Italian Renaissance: that images and colour enhance both *creativity* and *memory*, as well as being *easier* and more *enjoyable* than regular diary systems.

The Universal Personal Organiser *reflects you*, and gives you the *freedom* to perform at your highest potential. The Universal Personal Organiser is made of materials that are to the *highest quality*, using the best leathers and paper available.

The Universal Personal Organiser is designed to help you manage the four main areas of life: *health* (mental, physical and emotional); *family; creativity;* and *wealth*.

The Universal Personal Organiser, in so doing, allows you to organise your past, present and future in a manner that is both *enjoyable* and *fun*.

The Universal Personal Organiser's pages and partitions have been designed to enable you to get a comprehensive perspective on your *yearly plan*, your *monthly* and *weekly plans*, and your *daily plan*, using the new *24 hour diary clock, Mind Mapping*, and *Use Both Sides of Your Brain*.

4. BUZAN TRAINING COURSES

Courses are prepared for:
- ▶ Governments
- ▶ Corporations
- ▶ Schools and universities
- ▶ Private groups and organisations
- ▶ Foundations
- ▶ Children
- ▶ Families
- ▶ Senior citizens

The courses are based on the following books by Tony Buzan:
- ▶ *Use Both Sides of Your Brain*
- ▶ *Use Your Perfect Memory*
- ▶ *Make the Most of Your Mind*
- ▶ *Master Your Memory*
- ▶ *Speed (and Range) Reading*
- ▶ *The Brain User's Guide*
- ▶ *Universal Personal Organiser*

The courses emphasise:
- ▶ Mind Mapping
- ▶ Memory skills—advanced
- ▶ Speed reading—advanced
- ▶ Planning
- ▶ Learning to read
- ▶ Creativity
- ▶ Presentation skills
- ▶ Work/study skills
- ▶ Corporate and family brain training
- ▶ The ageing brain
- ▶ Managing change
- ▶ Personal and time management
- ▶ Especially tailored courses

For enquiries, please contact The Buzan Centre, Inc.

5. FOR FURTHER INFORMATION ON:

- ▶ Training courses based on Tony Buzan's methods
- ▶ Co-ordination of The Brain Club
- ▶ Supportive books, tapes and educational products contact:

Buzan Centres   **(800) Y MIND MAP**
415 Federal Highway   **FAX: (407) 845-3210**
Lake Park, FL 33403
(407) 881-0188

Please send a stamped, self-addressed envelope for your reply.

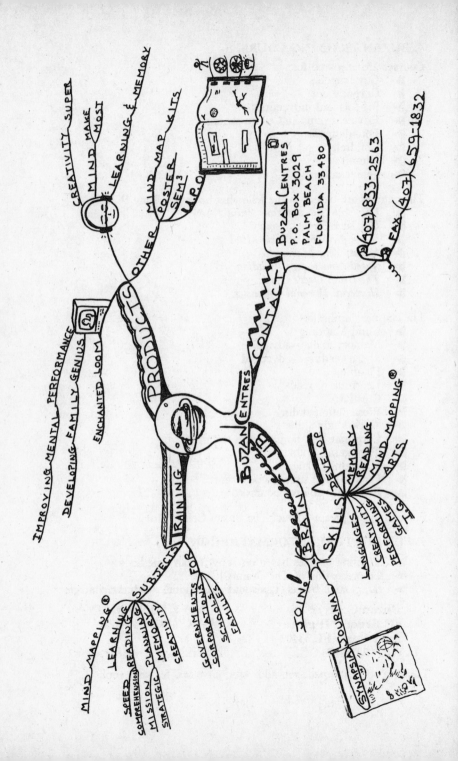

BIBLIOGRAPHY

Atkinson, Richard C., and Shiffrin, Richard M. 'The Control of Short-term Memory.' *Scientific American*, August 1971.

Baddeley, Alan D. *The Psychology of Memory*. New York: Harper & Row, 1976.

Borges, Jorge Luis. *Fictions* (especially *Funes, the Memorious*). London: Weidenfeld & Nicolson, 1962.

Brown, Mark. *Memory Matters*. Newton Abbot: David & Charles, 1977.

Brown, R., and McNeil, D. 'The "Tip-of-the-Tongue" Phenomenon.' *Journal of Verbal Learning and Verbal Behaviour* 5, pp. 325–37.

Buzan, Tony. *The Brain User's Guide*. New York: E. P. Dutton, 1983.

Buzan, Tony. *Make the Most of Your Mind*. Cambridge: Colt Books, 1977. London: Pan, 1981.

Buzan, Tony. *Master your Memory*. Newton Abbot: David & Charles, 1988, revised edition 1989.

Buzan, Tony. *Use Your Head*. London: BBC, 1974.

Buzan, Tony. *Use your Memory*. London: BBC, 1989.

Ebbinghaus, H. *Über das Gedächtnis*. Leipzig: Duncker, 1885.

Gelb, Michael. *Present Yourself*. London: Aurum Press, 1988.

Haber, Ralph N. 'How We Remember What We See.' *Scientific American*, p. 105, May 1970.

Howe, J. A., and Godfrey, J. *Student Note-Taking As An Aid to Learning*. Exeter: Exeter University Teaching Services, 1977.

Howe, M. J. A. 'Using Students' Notes to Examine the Role of the Individual Learner in Acquiring Meaningful Subject Matter.' *Journal of Educational Research* 64, pp. 61–3.

Hunt, E., and Love, T. 'How Good Can Memory Be?' *Coding Processes in Human Memory*, pp. 237–60, edited by A. W. Melton and E. Martin. Washington, DC: Winston/Wiley, 1972.

Hunter, I. M. L. 'An Exceptional Memory.' *British Journal of Psychology* 68, pp. 155–64, 1977.

Keyes, Daniel. *The Minds of Billy Milligan.* New York: Random House, 1981.

Loftus, E. F. *Eyewitness Testimony.* Cambridge, Mass.: Harvard University Press, 1979.

Luria, A. R. *The Mind of a Mnemonist.* London: Jonathan Cape, 1969.

Penfield, W., and Perot, P. 'The Brain's Record of Auditory and Visual Experience: A Final Summary and Discussion.' *Brain* 86, pp. 595–702.

Penfield, W., and Roberts, L. *Speech and Brain-Mechanisms.* Princeton, NJ: Princeton University Press, 1959.

Penry, J. *Looking at Faces and Remembering Them: A Guide to Facial Identification.* London: Elek Books, 1971.

Ruger, H. A., and Bussenius, C. E. *Memory.* New York: Teachers College Press, 1913.

Russell, Peter. *The Brain Book.* London: Routledge & Kegan Paul, 1979.

Standing, Lionel. 'Learning 10,000 Pictures.' *Quarterly Journal of Experimental Psychology* 25, pp. 207–22.

Stratton, George M. 'The Mnemonic Feat of the "Shass Pollak",' *Physiological Review* 24, pp. 244–7.

Suzuki, S. *Nurtured by Love: a New Approach to Education.* New York: Exposition Press, 1969.

Thomas, E. J. 'The Variation of Memory with Time for Information Appearing During a Lecture.' *Studies in Adult Education*, pp. 57–62, April 1972.

Tulving, E. 'The Effects of Presentation and Recall of Materials in Free-Recall Learning.' *Journal of Verbal Learning and Verbal Behaviour* 6, pp. 175–84.

von Restorff, H. 'Über die Wirkung von Bereichsbildungen im Spurenfeld.' *Psychologische Forschung* 18, pp. 299–342.

Wagner, D. 'Memories of Morocco: the influence of age, schooling and environment on memory.' *Cognitive Psychology* 10, pp. 1–28, 1978.

Yates, F. A. *The Art of Memory.* London: Routledge & Kegan Paul, 1966.

INDEX